# Workshop on Synchronic and Diachronic Approaches to Analyzing Technical Language

# (SADAATL 2014)



**Held at COLING 2014**

## Dublin, Ireland
## 24 August 2014

ISBN: 978-1-63439-228-0

**Printed from e-media with permission by:**

Curran Associates, Inc.
57 Morehouse Lane
Red Hook, NY 12571



Printed by Curran Associates, Inc. (2014)



Association for Computational Linguistics
209 N. Eighth Street
Stroudsburg, Pennsylvania 18360

Phone: 1-570-476-8006
Fax: 1-570-476-0860

acl@aclweb.org

**Additional copies of this publication are available from:**

Curran Associates, Inc.
57 Morehouse Lane
Red Hook, NY 12571 USA
Phone: 845-758-0400
Fax: 845-758-2634
Email: curran@proceedings.com
Web: www.proceedings.com

# Introduction

The Coling 2014 Workshop on Synchronic and Diachronic Approaches to Analyzing Technical Language was held on August 24, 2014 in Dublin Ireland.

Technology is the application of knowledge to practical pursuits. Information relevant to technology is the subject of various types of documents, including: scholarly publications (journals, conference proceedings, abstracts, grant applications, textbooks); legal documents (patents, contracts, legislation); and more public venues (magazines, webpages, blogs, financial reports). Interest in the automatic classification of technical documents has recently been growing and Natural Language Processing is a major component of such classification systems.

Presented at this workshop were six regular papers and two invited talks on various topics connected to the linguistic analysis of technical language including work on terminology, citations, Chinese-English Machine Translation, Sentiment Analysis, event extraction, literary analysis, named entity recognition, among other topics. Technical domains investigated included both patents and journal articles.

We thank the invited speakers, program committee, authors, Coling organizers and participants for a successful workshop.

Adam Meyers, Yifan He and Ralph Grishman

**Co-Chairs**

Adam Meyers, New York University, USA
Yifan He, New York University, USA
Ralph Grishman, New York University, USA

**Program Committee**

Olga Babko-Malaya, BAE Systems, USA
Josef van Genabith, DFKI, Germany
Kris Jack, Mendeley, UK
Min-Yen Kan, National University of Singapore, Singapore
Roman Kern, Know-Center, Austria
Arzucan Özgür, Bogazici University, Turkey
James Pustejovsky, Brandeis University, USA
Dragomir Radev, University of Michigan, USA
Ulrich Schäfer, DFKI, Germany
Simone Teufel, University of Cambridge, UK
Marc Verhagen, Brandeis University, USA
Nianwen Xue, Brandeis University, USA

**Invited Speakers**

Sophia Ananiadou, University of Manchester, UK
Simone Teufel, University of Cambridge, UK

# Table of Contents

*Investigating Context Parameters in Technology Term Recognition*
Behrang Q. Zadeh and Siegfried Handschuh . . . . . . . . . . . . . . . . . . . . . . . . . . . . . . . . . . . . . . . . . . . . . . . 1

*Jargon-Term Extraction by Chunking*
Adam Meyers, Zachary Glass, Angus Grieve-Smith, Yifan He, Shasha Liao and Ralph Grishman 11

*Ontology-based Technical Text Annotation*
François Lévy, Nadi Tomeh and Yue Ma . . . . . . . . . . . . . . . . . . . . . . . . . . . . . . . . . . . . . . . . . . . . . . . . . 21

*Extracting Aspects and Polarity from Patents*
Peter Anick, Marc Verhagen and James Pustejovsky . . . . . . . . . . . . . . . . . . . . . . . . . . . . . . . . . . . . . . . . . 31

*Pre-reordering Model of Chinese Special Sentences for Patent Machine Translation*
Renfen Hu, Zhiying Liu, Lijiao Yang and Yaohong Jin . . . . . . . . . . . . . . . . . . . . . . . . . . . . . . . . . . . . . 40

*A Study of Scientific Writing: Comparing Theoretical Guidelines with Practical Implementation*
Mark Kröll, Gunnar Schulze and Roman Kern . . . . . . . . . . . . . . . . . . . . . . . . . . . . . . . . . . . . . . . . . . . . . 48

# Program

| | |
|---|---|
| 9:30 | Intro |
| 9:45 | Invited Talk by Sophia Ananiadou |
| 10:30 | Coffee Break |
| 11:00 | *Investigating Context Parameters in Technology Term Recognition*<br>Behrang Q. Zadeh and Siegfried Handschuh |
| 11:30 | *Jargon-Term Extraction by Chunking*<br>Adam Meyers, Zachary Glass, Angus Grieve-Smith, Yifan He, Shasha Liao and Ralph Grishman |
| 12:00 | *Ontology-based Technical Text Annotation*<br>François Lévy, Nadi Tomeh and Yue Ma |
| 12:30 | Lunch Break |
| 14:15 | Invited Talk by Simone Teufel |
| 15:00 | Coffee Break |
| 15:30 | *Extracting Aspects and Polarity from Patents*<br>Peter Anick, Marc Verhagen and James Pustejovsky |
| 16:00 | *Pre-reordering Model of Chinese Special Sentences for Patent Machine Translation*<br>Renfen Hu, Zhiying Liu, Lijiao Yang and Yaohong Jin |
| 16:30 | *A Study of Scientific Writing: Comparing Theoretical Guidelines with Practical Implementation*<br>Mark Kröll, Gunnar Schulze and Roman Kern |
| 17:00 | Closing |

# Investigating Context Parameters in Technology Term Recognition

**Behrang Q. Zadeh and Siegfried Handschuh**[*†]
[*]Insight Centre of Data Analytics
National University of Ireland, Galway
[†]Department of Computer Science and Mathematics
University of Passau, Germany
{behrang.qasemizadeh, siegfried.handschuh}@insight-centre.org

## Abstract

We propose and evaluate the task of technology term recognition: a method to extract technology terms at a synchronic level from a corpus of scientific publications. The proposed method is built on the principles of terminology extraction and distributional semantics. It is realized as a regression task in a vector space model. In this method, candidate terms are first extracted from text. Subsequently, using the random indexing technique, the extracted candidate terms are represented as vectors in a Euclidean vector space of reduced dimensionality. These vectors are derived from the frequency of co-occurrences of candidate terms and words in windows of text surrounding candidate terms in the input corpus (context window). The constructed vector space and a set of manually tagged technology terms (reference vectors) in a $k$-nearest neighbours regression framework is then used to identify terms that signify technology concepts. We examine a number of factors that play roles in the performance of the proposed method, i.e. the configuration of context windows, neighborhood size ($k$) selection, and reference vector size.

## 1 Introduction

Technology terms and their corresponding concepts are part and parcel of any system that tries to capture competitive technological intelligence (QasemiZadeh, 2010; Newman et al., 2014). We propose a method of technology term recognition (TTR) at a synchronic level, i.e., the identification of terms that correspond to technological concepts from a corpus of scientific publications. TTR can be viewed as a kind of automatic term recognition (ATR) task. The input of ATR is a large collection of documents, i.e. a domain-specific corpus, and the output is a terminological resource. The generated terminological resource embraces terms that signify a wide spectrum of concepts in domain knowledge represented by the input corpus. The extracted terms and their corresponding concepts, however, can be further organized in several categories; each category characterizes a group of 'similar' concepts (e.g. technology) in domain knowledge.[1] TTR, therefore, goes beyond ATR and targets a subset of terms that characterizes the category of technological concepts in domain knowledge (Figure 1).

Establishing a precise definition of technology—and subsequently finding its corresponding terms—is a fundamental problem studied in philosophy of science. The most simplistic definition of technology, perhaps, can be found in a dictionary. For example, Oxford dictionary defines technology as the 'application of scientific knowledge for practical purposes'. As to our understanding, technology terms signal concepts that involve processes—a series of actions taken in order to achieve a particular goal—e.g. as manifested in practical applications of a research. Consequently, technology terms should not be confused with other categories of terms, e.g. terms that signify research subjects or problems.[2] For example, in computational linguistics literature, both 'language resource' and 'natural language processing' are



[1]Or, contrariwise, a group of similar concepts can form a category.

[2]Even though, these category of terms are strongly correlated. For instance, a technology may provide a solution for a research problem and can be defined in the scope of a research subject. Therefore, it is important to note that a research problem or a research subject is not a technology.



*Proceedings of SADAATL 2014*, pages 1–10,
Dublin, Ireland, August 24, 2014.

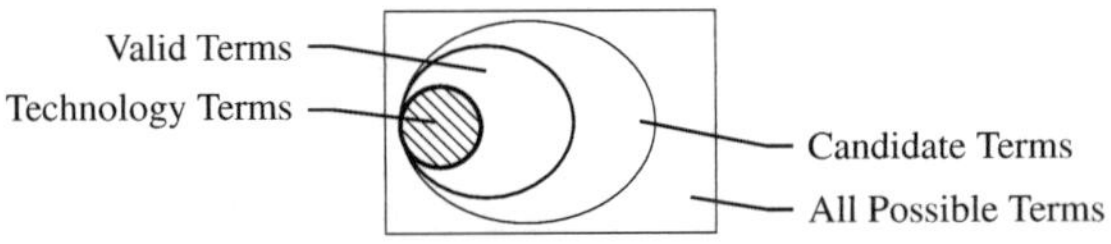


Figure 1: A Venn diagram that illustrates relationships between candidate terms, valid terms and technology terms. ATR targets the identification of valid terms amongst candidate terms. TTR, however, targets the identification of technology terms amongst candidate terms, i.e. a subset of valid terms.

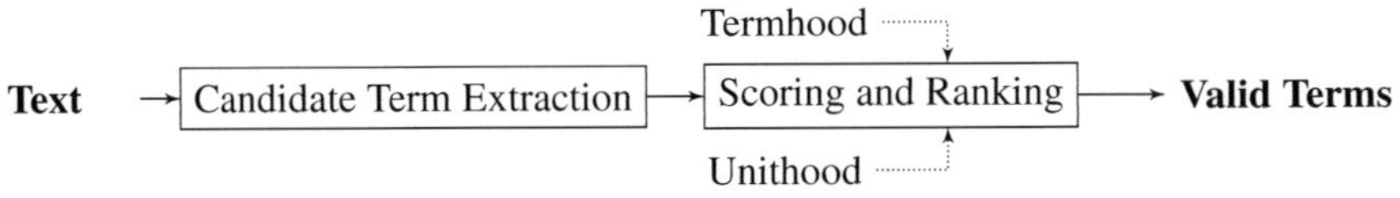


Figure 2: Prevalent architecture of the terminology mining methods.

valid terms; however, we only recognize the latter as a valid technology term.[3] In this example, 'language resource' signals artefacts such as lexicons and corpora. Although the process of creating these artefacts involves several technologies, we do not consider them—and subsequently the term 'language resource'—as technology.

In the absence of an analytical answer to the question 'what is technology?', we suggest exploiting the context of terms in order to identify technology terms among them. We believe that technology terms tend to appear in similar linguistic contexts. By extending Harris's (1954) distributional hypothesis, we claim that the context of (previously) known technology terms can be modelled and used in order to identify new unknown technology terms. We thus take a distributional approach to the problem of technology term recognition. Consequently, we tie the context of terms to their meaning by quantification of their distributional similarities. We employ vector spaces to model such distributional similarities (Turney and Pantel, 2010). Consequently, the proposed method for TTR is realized as a term classification task in a vector space model (VSM).

The proposed method employs the prevalent mechanism of terminology extraction in the form of a two-step procedure: candidate term extraction followed by term scoring and ranking (Figure 2). Candidate term extraction deals with the term formation and the extraction of term candidates. We employ a linguistic filtering based on part-of-speech (PoS) tag sequences for the extraction of candidate terms. Subsequent to candidate term extraction, a scoring procedure—which can be seen as a semantic weighting mechanism—is employed to indicate how likely it is that a candidate term is a technology term. As suggested in Figure 2, the scoring procedure in ATR usually combines scores that are known as *termhood* and *unithood*. Unithood indicates the degree to which a sequence of tokens can be combined to form a complex term (a lexical unit that is made of more than one token). Unithood is, thus, a measure of the syntagmatic relation between the constituents of complex terms: a lexical association measure to identify collocations.[4] Termhood, on the other hand, 'is the degree to which a stable lexical unit is related to some domain-specific concepts' (Kageura and Umino, 1996). It characterizes a *paradigmatic* relation between lexical units—either simple (made of one token) or complex terms—and the communicative context that verbalizes domain-concepts. In this paper, in order to simplify the evaluation framework, we assume that the PoS-based approach to candidate term extraction implicitly characterizes the unithood score. The focus is thus on the termhood measure.

We devise a termhood measure to distinguish technology terms from the set of extracted candidate terms. We assume that the association of a term to a technology concept (i.e. what termhood determines) is a kind of paradigmatic relation that can be characterized using the syntagmatic relations of the term and its co-occurred, surrounding words in a context window (Figure 3). Words appeared in context win-

[3]Please note that 'natural language processing', in its alternative sense, can also signal a research subject as well as a research problem.

[4]See Evert (2004) on the application of lexical association measures for the identification of collocations.

··· discuss challenges that arise when employing current **Information Extraction** technology to discover knowledge in text ···

··· picture of the impact of using different **Information Extraction** methods for the offline construction of knowledge ···

··· on the development of the technology of **Information Extraction** has been stimulated by the Message Understanding ···

Figure 3: Example of a context window of size 3 that extends around terms: words that are placed in rectangles. In this example, this context-window is shown for the occurrences of the term 'information extraction' in three different sentences.

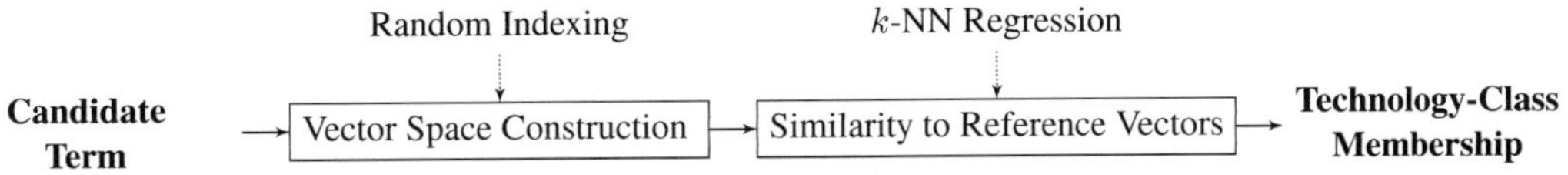


Figure 4: Method for measuring the association of a candidate term to the category of technology terms.

dows are represented by the elements of the standard basis of a vector space.[5] The frequency of words in context windows of a candidate term (in the whole corpus) then determines the coordinates of the vector that represent the candidate term. To avoid the *curse of dimensionality*, the VSMs are constructed at reduced dimensionality using the random indexing technique . In this VSM, we characterize the category of technology terms using a set of reference terms, i.e. previously known technology terms. Consequently, the proximity of vectors that represent candidate terms to the vectors that represent reference terms determines the association of candidate terms to the category of technology terms. This association is measured using a $k$-nearest neighbours ($k$-nn) regression algorithm. Figure 4 illustrates the method.

In the proposed technique, finding context window's properties that best characterize technology terms is the major research concern that should be investigated. These properties are the size of the co-occurrence region, the position of a term in the context window and the direction in which the neighbourhood is extended (see Lenci, 2008). To find the most discriminative context window, we construct several VSMs; each VSM represents a context window of a certain configuration (i.e. size, direction and the word order information). We then examine the discriminative power of context windows by reporting the performance of the $k$-nn regression algorithm in these VSMs. Furthermore, to examine the role of the number of reference vectors in the performance of the classification task, we repeat these experiments using various numbers of reference vectors. We report the results of similar evaluation methodology, however, using a $k$-nn voting algorithm in Zadeh and Handschuh (2014b).

In the rest of this paper, we first detail the evaluation framework in Section 2: the employed corpus for the evaluation in Section 2.1, the construction of vector spaces in Section 2.2, the scoring procedure in Section 2.3 and the evaluation methodology in Section 2.4. Subsequently, we report the observed results in Section 3 and conclude in Section 4.

## 2 Setting the Scene

### 2.1 Evaluation Corpus

In order to evaluate the proposed method, we employ the ACL anthology reference corpus (ACL ARC) (Bird et al., 2008) and the ACL reference dataset for terminology extraction and classification (AC RD-TEC) (Zadeh and Handschuh, 2014a).[6] The ACL ARC has been developed with the aim of providing a platform for benchmarking methods of scholarly document processing. It consists of 10,922 articles that were published between 1965 to 2006 in the domain of computational linguistics. These articles are digitized and enriched with bibliography metadata. The provided resources in the ACL ARC consist of three layers: (a) source publications in portable document format (PDF), (b) automatically extracted text from the articles and (c) bibliographic metadata and citation network. Each of the articles in the collection is assigned to a unique identifier that indicates the source (e.g. journal or conference)

[5]That is, informally, each dimension of the vector space.

[6]The ACL RD-TEC can be obtained from the European Language Resources Association, catalogue ELRA-T0375.

| Type | Token | Sentence | Paragraph | Section | Publication |
|---|---|---|---|---|---|
| 704,085 | 36,729,513 | 1,564,430 | 510,366 | 92,935 | 10,922 |

Table 1: Summary statistics of the dataset derived from automatic processing of the ACL ARC.

| | Total# | Length = 1 | Length = 2 | Length = 3 | Length = 4 | Length = 5 |
|---|---|---|---|---|---|---|
| **Technology Terms** | 13,841 | 759 | 8,674 | 3,826 | 539 | 43 |
| **Valid Terms** | 22,044 | 1,503 | 14,148 | 5,680 | 659 | 54 |
| **Invalid Terms** | 61,758 | 15,887 | 33,474 | 11,016 | 1,210 | 171 |
| **Total Annotated** | 83,802 | 17,390 | 47,622 | 16,696 | 1,869 | 225 |

Table 2: Summary statistics of the annotated candidate terms.

and the date (e.g. 1999, 2006, etc.) of publication.

The ACL RD-TEC is a spin-off of the ACL ARC corpus. It further enriches the ACL ARC metadata using automatic and manual annotations. The ACL RD-TEC employed the SectLabel module of Luong et al.'s (2010) ParsCit tool for the automatic identification of logical text sections in ACL ARC's raw text files. The resulting segmented text units are cleansed using a set of heuristics; for instance, broken words and text segments are joined, footnotes and captions are removed, and sections are organised into paragraphs. Text sections are further segmented into PoS-tagged sentences and each linguistically well-defined unit, e.g. types (i.e. PoS-tagged and lemmatized words), sentences, paragraphs and (sub)sections, is assigned to a unique identifier. These text units are stored and presented in inverted index files, in a tab-separated format. Hence, text units can be easily traced back to the contexts and, eventually, publications that they appeared in. Table 1 shows the statistics of text segments in the dataset.

The ACL RD-TEC consists of manual annotations that can be used for the evaluation of ATR and term classification tasks. In its current release, more than 80,000 lexical units[7] are annotated as either valid or invalid terms. For a given lexical form $t$, if $t$ refers to a significant concept in the computational linguistics domain, it is annotated as valid.[8] Examples of valid terms are 'natural language' and 'terminology'. In addition, valid terms are classified as those that can signal a technology concept. Technology terms indicate a method or a process that is employed to accomplish a task; examples of these terms are 'parsing' and 'information retrieval', and more delicate terms such as 'linear interpolation'.

Similar to the valid terms, terms that are annotated as technology terms do not exclusively belong to this class. For example, 'computational linguistics' is a lexical form that can be classified as a technology term, e.g., in '$\cdots$ promising area of application of *computational linguistics* techniques$\cdots$'. However, it can also signal other concepts such as a scientific discipline as well as a community, e.g., in '$\cdots$ theoretical work in *computational linguistics*$\cdots$' and '$\cdots$ pursued by the *computational linguistics* community $\cdots$', respectively.

As reported in Zadeh and Handschuh (2014a), the observed agreement between 4 participants in the manual annotation of technology terms from a small set of randomly selected candidate terms is 0.828; the obtained Cohen's kappa coefficient for inter annotator agreement is 0.627. Table 2 shows the current statistics of the annotated terms.

### 2.2 Construction of Vector Space Models using Random Indexing

We employ random indexing (RI) for the construction of the VSMs (Kanerva et al., 2000). For a corpus of a relatively small size, the context of terms can be represented and efficiently examined with the help of conventional vector space construction methods. The vector space is first constructed and then it may be followed by a dimensionality reduction technique. However, as the corpus grows and the number of elements that are employed for context definition increases, due to the high dimensionality of the vector space (orders of millions), these algorithms may suffer from low computational performance. RI is an approach that alleviates this problem by combining the construction of a vector space and the dimension reduction process. RI is based on normal random projection. It thus guarantees that

[7] A lexical unit is defined as a single token, part of a word, a word or a combination of these.

[8] However, it is not guaranteed that all the occurrences of $t$ in the corpus are valid terms.

the relative Euclidean distance between vectors, as well as their cosine similarity, in the original high-dimensional vector space is preserved in the vector space that is constructed at a reduced dimensionality. The vector space construction is a two-step procedure: construction of (a) *index vectors* followed by the construction of (b) *context vectors*.

In the first step, each context element (i.e. a PoS-tagged word in a context window) is assigned *exactly* to one *index vector*. Index vectors are high-dimensional randomly generated vectors, in which most of the elements are set to 0 and only a few to 1 and $-1$.[9] Once an index vector is generated and assigned to a context element, this information is stored so that it can be retrieved and used for later analysis. In the second step, the construction of *context vectors*, each candidate term is assigned to a vector of which all elements are zero. This context vector has the same dimension as the index vectors. For each co-occurrence of a candidate term (represented by the context vector $\vec{v}_{t_i}$) and a context element (represented by the index vector $\vec{r}_{w_j}$) in the corpus, the context vector for the candidate term is accumulated by the index vector of the context element, i.e. $\vec{v}_{t_i} = \vec{v}_{t_i} + \vec{r}_{w_j}$. The corpus is scanned for all the co-occurrences of candidate terms and context elements and the context vectors are updated to reflect these co-occurrences. The result is a VSM that is constructed directly in the reduced dimensionality and represents candidate terms using the defined context.

For instance, in the example given in Figure 3, the term 'information extraction' is assigned to a context vector. If a context window of size 3 that extends in both directions of candidate terms and discards word order information is employed, then each unique word in the rectangles, e.g. has, current, technology, the, been, etc., is assigned to a randomly generated index vector. The context vector is then obtained by the accumulation of these index vectors. If the word order information is encoded, then the appearance of each word at a certain position in the context window must be assigned to a unique index vector. As a result, in the given example in Figure 3, the word 'technology' in the first sentence (position 1 after target term) and the third sentence (position 2 before the target term) is assigned to two different index vectors, each uniquely represents the word 'technology' at these positions.

In order to employ random indexing, two parameters must be decided: the dimensionality of the VSM and the number of non-zero elements. As described in Zadeh and Handschuh (2014c), using the provided proofs in Li et al. (2006), it can be verified that the dimensionality of RI-constructed VSMs is determined independently of the number of context elements $n$ (i.e. the original dimensionality of the vector space). It is, however, determined by the probability and the maximum expected amount of distortions in pairwise distances and the number of context vectors in the model (in logarithmic scale). The number of non-zero elements, on the other hand, is decided by the number of context elements and the sparseness of the VSM at the original high dimension ($\alpha$) as $O(\sqrt{\alpha n})$. Accordingly, in the reported experiment in this paper, we set the dimension of RI-constructed VSMs to 1800, which is large enough to make sure that the distances are preserved in the constructed VSMs. In our experimental setup using the contexts that are described in Section 2.4.1, the estimated non-reduced, original dimension of the vector space is between 700,000 and 7 million; [10] hence, we set 8 elements of index vectors to $\pm 1$.

## 2.3 Term Scoring Method: $k$-Nearest Neighbours Regression

We employ a standard $k$-nn regression method to assign scores to the extracted candidate terms. In this framework, context vectors that represent candidate terms are compared to those that represent a set of reference terms $R_s$. $R_s$ consists of both technology and non-technology terms that are manually tagged prior to the similarity measurement task. We employ the cosine similarity. For each candidate term $t$, terms in $R_s$ are sorted in descending order by their cosine similarity to $t$. We calculate the sum of the similarity of valid technology terms to $t$ in the top $k$ terms of this sorted list and consider it as a measurement of the technology-term class membership for $t$. As described later in Section 2.4.2, the

[9]This distribution of zero and $\pm 1$ elements in index vectors this leads to a Gaussian asymptotic distribution and consequently a Gaussian random projection matrix (see Zadeh and Handschuh, 2014c, for further explanation).

[10]In the defined contexts for our experiments, the original dimension of the vector space is determined by the number of types in the corpus, i.e. 700,000. This number increases when the word order information is also encoded. In the reported experiment, this number escalates to 7 million for a context window of size 5 that extends around the terms and encode word order information).

| #Term$_{Total}$ | #Term$_{Technology}$ | Average Length | $f$(Sentence) | $f$(Paragraph) | $f$(Section) | $f$(Document) |
|---|---|---|---|---|---|---|
| 3,490 | 1,596 | 2.037 | 1,696,201 | 1,264,616 | 870,574 | 346,000 |

Table 3: Summary statistics of the reference terms $R_s$. $f(x)$ denotes the accumulative frequency of occurrences of all the terms in $R_s$ in text segments of type $x$.

neighbourhood size $k$ is defined relative to the size of $R_s$.

As stated earlier, candidate terms are extracted from the ACL ARC corpus using a part-of-speech-based filtering technique. In this method, any sequence of tokens in the corpus that conforms to one of the predefined part-of-speech tag sequences is considered as a term candidate. By employing 31 different patterns of length 1 to 5, we extract 1.3 million candidate terms.[11] Using the $k$-nn regression described above, the technology-term class membership is calculated for all the candidate terms.

#### 2.3.1 Reference Term Formation

Prior to the $k$-nn regression task, we extract all the candidate terms which ended or collocated with the words 'technology' and 'technique' (in their lemmatized form). Examples of the extracted terms are 'unsupervised text categorization', 'basic estimation', 'bi-directional bottom-up' and 'boolean keyword'. These terms are then manually annotated as technology and non-technology terms. For example, in the list of terms given above, only 'unsupervised text categorization' is annotated as a technology term. The process resulted in a set of reference terms $R_s$ consisting of 3490 terms of which 1596 are annotated as technology terms (i.e. positive examples). The accumulative frequency of the occurrences of the extracted reference terms in the corpus are given in Table 3.

### 2.4 Evaluation Methodology

In the reported evaluation framework, the procedure described in Section 2.2 is performed to construct several vector spaces of various context configurations, which are described in Section 2.4.1. The described procedure for term scoring in Section 2.3 is then employed to assign scores to the extracted candidate terms in all the constructed vector spaces. In each experiment, candidate terms are sorted in descending order by their assigned scores. The proportion of technology terms in the list of the top $n$ terms (we start with 250 terms) is reported for the comparison of the performance of the evaluated context configurations. We further investigate the role of the neighbourhood size selection $k$ as well as the number of reference terms $R_s$ in the performance of the scoring task.

#### 2.4.1 Evaluated Context Parameters

In the reported evaluation, the terms' contexts are defined by the frequency of distinct PoS-tagged words that co-occurred with terms in a text window of limited size. We evaluate context windows that are configured with three parameters: direction, size and order.

The first parameter distinguishes context windows according to the direction in which they are expanded to collect the co-occurrence counts. The context window of a term is expanded (a) to the left-hand side of the term to count the co-occurrence counts of the term with its preceding words in each sentence of the corpus, (b) to the right-hand side to collect co-occurrences with the succeeding words or (c) around the term, i.e. in both left and right directions. The context windows are also configured by their size, i.e. the extent of terms' neighbourhood for counting the co-occurrences. As stated in Sahlgren (2008), an optimum size of a context window can only be found through experiments. However, he also suggests that if the goal is to capture a paradigmatic relation (such as the one proposed here), then narrow context windows outperform wide context windows. As a result, in our experiments we limit the size of context windows $w$ to $1 \leq w \leq 5$. For the context windows that expand around terms, we extend the context region symmetrically in both directions. As stated earlier, Figure 3 illustrates a context window of size 3 that extends around terms.

Some research suggests that the sequential order of words expresses information about the grammatical behaviour of words and, therefore, the inclusion of this information in a distributional model enhances

[11]The extracted candidate terms are included in the ACL RD-TEC.

the performance. We investigate the impact of word order information on the performance of the suggested task. Capturing word order information requires distinguishing the location of words in context windows. To attain this goal in the random indexing technique, as stated earlier in Section 2.2, the appearance of the same word in different positions in a context window is recognized by assigning the word to several index vectors, each index vector denotes the appearance of the word in certain position. Alternatively, the order of words (i.e. the position of a word in a context window) can be captured by shuffling their index vectors via a permutation function (Sahlgren et al., 2008).[12] In our implementation, a circular shift function serves as the permutation function. Accordingly, if $m$ is the number of tokens after/before a target term and a word in a context window, then the index vector of the word is shifted $m$ times circularly to the right/left before its accumulation to the target term's context vector.

### 2.4.2 Evaluated Parameters of $k$-Nearest Neighbours Regression

In addition to different configurations of context windows, we investigate the role of two other parameters in the performance of the proposed $k$-nn-based method: the neighbourhood size $k$ and the number of reference vectors $|R_s|$. The performance of $k$-nn is largely dependent on the value of $k$: a small value for $k$ leads to over-fitting, while a large neighbourhood estimation may reduce the discriminatory power of the classifier. The optimum $k$ is subject to the number of reference vectors and the underlying probability distribution of target instances in the vector space. The underlying probability distribution is unknown and difficult to estimate. Therefore, the optimal value of $k$ is usually obtained by an experimental method (Yang, 1999). Yang also suggests that the performance of the $k$-nn algorithm is relatively stable for a large range of $k$ values. Accordingly, we perform an empirical assessment by inspecting the output of the proposed method with respect to various values of $k$ that are defined in relation to $|R_s|$. The main objective of our experiment, however, is to examine whether the best-performing context configuration can be distinguished irrespective of the value of $k$. Accordingly, we report the performance of the scoring procedure when $k = \lfloor pR_s \rfloor$, for $p \in \{0.001, 0.005, 0.01, 0.1, 0.2\}$.

Building reference vectors $R_s$ is laborious; it entails a manual annotation of terms. It requires a domain expert to provide a list of representative technology terms (positive examples) and non-technology terms (negative examples) from the corpus that is being analyzed.[13] As a result, a $R_s$ of small size is often more desirable than a large one. In $k$-nn, a small $R_s$ is also desirable from the computational complexity point of view. However, using a large set of reference vectors often yields higher performance. As a result, the choice of the number of reference vectors $|R_s|$ is a trade-off between efficiency and performance. We thus compare the performance of the method for values of $|R_s| \in \{100, 200, 300, 600, 1100, 1600, 3200, 3490\}$. In each experiment, we made sure that the created $R_s$ has a balanced number of positive and negative examples; however, the terms are chosen randomly.

## 3 Observed Evaluation Results

Table 4 reports the observed results in the first set of experiments. We start to score all the candidate terms using the complete set of reference vectors, i.e. $|R_s| = 3490$. We perform the experiments for all the possible configurations of context windows, as described in Section 2.4. Each of these experiments are repeated for $k = \lfloor p|R_s| \rfloor$, for $p \in \{0.001, 0.005, 0.01, 0.1, 0.2\}$. In these experiments, therefore, the assessed values of $k$ are $\{3, 17, 34, 349, 698\}$. Table 4a and 4b shows the observed results in the constructed VSMs when the word order information is excluded and included, respectively. In both tables, columns show the observed proportion of technology terms in the top 250 terms in the list of candidate terms that are weighted using the proposed method; thus, the closer a number is to 1, the higher the performance. We suggest Frantzi et al.'s (1998) $c$-value score—a general ATR algorithm—for the baseline measure. The $c$-value score of a term is measured by its frequency in the corpus that is normalized by its length and the frequency of its occurrences in other longer terms as a nested term. In our experiment, the proportion of technology terms in the top 250 terms in the list of candidate terms that are weighted by the $c$-value score is $0.252$.

[12] Assuming that shuffling of index vectors is equivalent to generating a new one.

[13] Depending on the type of classification–regression technique, the negative examples may not be required.

| Context | | Value of p in k = $\lfloor p\lvert R_s\rvert \rfloor = \lfloor p \cdot 3400 \rfloor$ | | | | |
|---|---|---|---|---|---|---|
| Type | Size | 0.001 | 0.005 | 0.01 | 0.10 | 0.20 |
| Left | 1 | 0.264 | 0.592 | 0.596 | 0.580 | 0.536 |
| | 2 | 0.132 | 0.688 | 0.664 | 0.644 | 0.556 |
| | 3 | 0.376 | 0.688 | 0.696 | 0.592 | 0.512 |
| | 4 | 0.524 | 0.692 | 0.656 | 0.616 | 0.536 |
| | 5 | 0.636 | 0.660 | 0.660 | 0.580 | 0.504 |
| Right | 1 | 0.124 | 0.440 | 0.512 | 0.224 | 0.284 |
| | 2 | 0.628 | 0.688 | 0.288 | 0.380 | 0.360 |
| | 3 | 0.684 | 0.496 | 0.440 | 0.380 | 0.380 |
| | 4 | 0.596 | 0.664 | 0.340 | 0.456 | 0.412 |
| | 5 | 0.708 | 0.632 | 0.672 | 0.452 | 0.436 |
| Around | 1 | 0.440 | 0.748 | 0.744 | 0.608 | 0.616 |
| | 2 | 0.716 | 0.836 | 0.848 | 0.764 | 0.700 |
| | 3 | 0.760 | 0.840 | 0.816 | 0.696 | 0.664 |
| | 4 | 0.160 | 0.800 | 0.788 | 0.672 | 0.660 |
| | 5 | 0.144 | 0.748 | 0.740 | 0.660 | 0.660 |

(a) No Word Order Information

| Context | | Value of p in k = $\lfloor p\lvert R_s\rvert \rfloor = \lfloor p \cdot 3400 \rfloor$ | | | | |
|---|---|---|---|---|---|---|
| Type | Size | 0.001 | 0.005 | 0.01 | 0.10 | 0.20 |
| Left | 1 | 0.264 | 0.592 | 0.596 | 0.580 | 0.536 |
| | 2 | 0.128 | 0.660 | 0.644 | 0.588 | 0.524 |
| | 3 | 0.344 | 0.676 | 0.652 | 0.544 | 0.448 |
| | 4 | 0.400 | 0.648 | 0.664 | 0.524 | 0.436 |
| | 5 | 0.448 | 0.632 | 0.640 | 0.488 | 0.408 |
| Right | 1 | 0.124 | 0.440 | 0.512 | 0.224 | 0.284 |
| | 2 | 0.696 | 0.736 | 0.788 | 0.316 | 0.368 |
| | 3 | 0.720 | 0.388 | 0.688 | 0.304 | 0.328 |
| | 4 | 0.580 | 0.376 | 0.600 | 0.324 | 0.328 |
| | 5 | 0.768 | 0.384 | 0.552 | 0.328 | 0.328 |
| Around | 1 | 0.376 | 0.768 | 0.804 | 0.704 | 0.624 |
| | 2 | 0.796 | 0.836 | 0.824 | 0.644 | 0.608 |
| | 3 | 0.760 | 0.828 | 0.808 | 0.636 | 0.572 |
| | 4 | 0.784 | 0.808 | 0.776 | 0.612 | 0.540 |
| | 5 | 0.784 | 0.808 | 0.756 | 0.580 | 0.516 |

(b) Encoded Word Order Information

Table 4: The observed results from the performed evaluations. The number columns show the proportion of technology terms in the top 250 terms for various values of $k$.

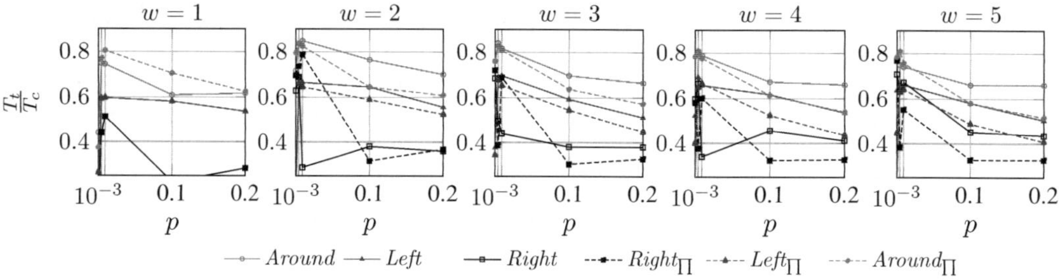


Figure 5: The performance of various context configurations over various neighbourhood sizes of $k = \lfloor p\lvert R_s\rvert \rfloor$. $\lvert\frac{T_t}{T_c}\rvert$ denotes the proportion of technology terms in the top 250 terms that are sorted by their assigned scores. $\prod$ denotes context types that encode word order information. The minimum value of $\lvert\frac{T_t}{T_c}\rvert$ axis is set to 0.252, i.e. our baseline. The baseline is the proportion of technology terms in the top 250 terms in the list of candidate terms that are weighted using the $c$-value technique.

As shown in Figure 5, weighting terms in the VSMs that are built using context windows that extend in both directions of candidate terms (i.e. *around* candidate terms) outperforms VSMs constructed by other types of context windows. In addition, as can also be verified in Table 4, the results from narrow context windows ($1 \leq w \leq 3$) are more desirable than those from wide context windows ($w \geq 3$). However, in contrast to our previous experiments, in which we employed an unweighted $k$-nn *voting classification* framework (Zadeh and Handschuh, 2014b), encoding word order information in the constructed VSMs does not necessarily improve the results. It is important to note that for different values of $k$, although the overall performance of the TTR method changes, the relative performance of the employed context windows with respect to each other is, nearly, constant. Therefore, we conclude that the best-performing context type, thus VSM, can be decided independently of the value of $k$: a result similar to that reported in Zadeh and Handschuh (2014b) for an unweighted $k$-nn voting classification.

### 3.1 Inspecting the Effect of Reference Vector Size

We are interested in studying the effect of reference vector size, i.e. $\lvert R_s\rvert$, on the overall performance of the technology term recognition task. In this set of experiments, we limit our evaluation to the best-performing context window in the previous evaluation task, i.e. the context window that extends *around* candidate terms. We repeat the scoring process for $\lvert R_s\rvert \in \{100, 200, 300, 600, 1600, 3490\}$. Similar to the previous set of experiments, we define and express the neighbourhood size ($k$) with respect to the

| | | the neighbourhood size (k) | | | | | |
|---|---|---|---|---|---|---|---|
| | | | Value of p in k = $\lfloor p\|R_s\| \rfloor$ | | | | |
| | w | k = 1 | 0.001 | 0.005 | 0.01 | 0.10 | 0.20 |
| $\|R_s\| = 100$ | 1 | 0.194 | 0.194 | 0.194 | 0.194 | 0.458 | 0.482 |
| | 2 | 0.228 | 0.228 | 0.228 | 0.228 | 0.466 | 0.490 |
| | 3 | 0.276 | 0.276 | 0.276 | 0.276 | 0.440 | 0.472 |
| | 4 | 0.076 | 0.076 | 0.076 | 0.076 | 0.470 | 0.488 |
| | 5 | 0.016 | 0.016 | 0.016 | 0.016 | 0.486 | 0.448 |
| $\|R_s\| = 300$ | 1 | 0.352 | 0.352 | 0.352 | 0.428 | 0.538 | 0.526 |
| | 2 | 0.390 | 0.390 | 0.390 | 0.492 | 0.646 | 0.638 |
| | 3 | 0.450 | 0.450 | 0.450 | 0.532 | 0.592 | 0.566 |
| | 4 | 0.020 | 0.020 | 0.020 | 0.382 | 0.584 | 0.590 |
| | 5 | 0.034 | 0.034 | 0.034 | 0.004 | 0.586 | 0.592 |
| $\|R_s\| = 1600$ | 1 | 0.958 | 0.958 | 0.484 | 0.670 | 0.590 | 0.542 |
| | 2 | 0.958 | 0.958 | 0.718 | 0.710 | 0.660 | 0.612 |
| | 3 | 0.958 | 0.958 | 0.674 | 0.702 | 0.592 | 0.574 |
| | 4 | 0.216 | 0.216 | 0.616 | 0.676 | 0.590 | 0.546 |
| | 5 | 0.502 | 0.502 | 0.368 | 0.570 | 0.566 | 0.552 |

| | | the neighbourhood size (k) | | | | | |
|---|---|---|---|---|---|---|---|
| | | | Value of p in k = $\lfloor p\|R_s\| \rfloor$ | | | | |
| | w | k = 1 | 0.001 | 0.005 | 0.01 | 0.10 | 0.20 |
| $\|R_s\| = 200$ | 1 | 0.322 | 0.322 | 0.322 | 0.348 | 0.516 | 0.480 |
| | 2 | 0.304 | 0.304 | 0.304 | 0.414 | 0.598 | 0.570 |
| | 3 | 0.378 | 0.378 | 0.378 | 0.466 | 0.504 | 0.468 |
| | 4 | 0.024 | 0.024 | 0.024 | 0.242 | 0.510 | 0.462 |
| | 5 | 0.040 | 0.040 | 0.040 | 0.012 | 0.516 | 0.472 |
| $\|R_s\| = 600$ | 1 | 0.678 | 0.678 | 0.426 | 0.514 | 0.556 | 0.526 |
| | 2 | 0.632 | 0.632 | 0.556 | 0.568 | 0.658 | 0.608 |
| | 3 | 0.652 | 0.652 | 0.534 | 0.488 | 0.604 | 0.550 |
| | 4 | 0.040 | 0.040 | 0.006 | 0.476 | 0.522 | 0.536 |
| | 5 | 0.088 | 0.088 | 0.014 | 0.234 | 0.526 | 0.530 |
| $\|R_s\| = 3490$ | 1 | 0.956 | 0.362 | 0.670 | 0.666 | 0.546 | 0.526 |
| | 2 | 0.956 | 0.624 | 0.722 | 0.734 | 0.608 | 0.586 |
| | 3 | 0.956 | 0.628 | 0.716 | 0.692 | 0.574 | 0.534 |
| | 4 | 0.992 | 0.118 | 0.698 | 0.682 | 0.550 | 0.528 |
| | 5 | 0.992 | 0.124 | 0.646 | 0.654 | 0.548 | 0.534 |

Table 5: The observed results, i.e. the proportion of technology terms in the list of top 500 candidate terms, for various sizes of the reference vectors set ($|R_s|$) and the neighbourhood size ($k$) for the context window that extends around the terms; $w$ denotes the size of context window.

size of the reference vectors ($|R_s|$), i.e. $k = \lfloor p|R_s| \rfloor$, for $p \in \{0.001, 0.005, 0.01, 0.1, 0.2\}$. In addition, we report the results for to the nearest-neighbour algorithm, i.e. when $k = 1$. For $|R_s| < 1000$ and $p = 0.001$ that results to $k = \lfloor 0.001|R_s| \rfloor = 0$, we set $k = 1$. In these cases, thus, the reported results for $k = \lfloor p|R_s| \rfloor$ is equivalent to the results reported for $k = 1$.

Table 5 reports the observed results: the proportion of technology terms in the top 500 terms in the list of candidate terms. First, these results suggest that the optimum value of $p$ in $k = \lfloor p|R_s| \rfloor$, and thus $k$, depends on $|R_s|$. If $|R_s|$ is small, a larger neighborhood performs better than a smaller neighborhood. Inversely, if $|R_s|$ is large enough, a small neighbourhood shows higher performance than a large neighborhood. Second, a small neighbourhood is sensitive to the size of context window $w$ (and perhaps the presence of noise), specifically when $|R_s|$ is small. As an example, for $|R_s| = 600$ and $k = 1$, if $w \geq 4$, then the performance drops sharply. Therefore, the performance of large neighbourhoods can be more stable than the performance of small neighbourhoods. Lastly, when $|R_s|$ reaches 1600 (a certain threshold), there is no significant increase in the performance of the algorithm. In this case, the nearest-neighbour algorithm outperforms the $k$-nn method. We suggest that the obtained results from the nearest-neighbour method can be used as a heuristic-based strategy for the selection of the number of vectors in the $|R_|$. Accordingly, one can stop adding new vectors to $R_s$ when the obtained results from the nearest-neighbour method are above a certain threshold.

## 4 Conclusion

In this paper, we proposed a corpus-based, distributional method for the recognition of technology terms from a corpus of scientific publications. The method is established as a $k$-nn regression task in a Euclidean vector space, in which vectors are compared by their cosine similarity. This vector space represents the co-occurrence frequencies of candidate terms and words in a context window. We examined a number of factors that play roles in the performance of the proposed method.

In order to find the most discriminative models, we studied several configurations of the context window: its size, the direction in which it is extended, and the incorporation of the word order information. According to these experiments, context windows that collect co-occurrence frequencies in both sides of terms, in narrow context, i.e. the size of 2 or 3 words, outperform other context types. We observed that narrow context windows, irrespective of other variables in the model (i.e. the $k$ and the number of reference vectors), consistently show a performance higher than other context configurations. Therefore, we suggest that the best-performing context type can be decided independently of the value of $k$ and the reference vector size. We also reported an initial experiment that assessed the effect of the reference vector size on the performance of the system.

We performed our evaluations on the ACL ARC corpus. Apart from the proposed methodology and reported experiments, another outcome of the performed experiment is a relatively large set of annotated technology terms, i.e. the ACL RD-TEC. The annotated terms in the ACL RD-TEC can be easily mapped into the ACL ARC documents, thus, into a chronological order and in a citation network. As a result, the annotations resulting from the experiments reported in this paper can be used in tasks other than technology term recognition, e.g. citation analysis and technology forecasting.

The reported experiment can be extended in several ways. In this paper, we focused on the extraction of technology terms at the corpus level. It would be helpful to investigate the best-performing context configurations when the co-occurrences are collected from communicative contexts of other sizes than corpus, e.g. at a document level, similar to automatic keyphrase extraction tasks. It is also interesting to compare the performance of the $k$-nn instance-based algorithm with other learning techniques such as support vector machines. Last but not least, we are interested in re-evaluating the proposed method using metrics other than the top $n$ terms look-up in the sorted weighted list of terms. A comparison of the evaluation metrics could be an attractive research avenue.

## Acknowledgements

We thank the anonymous reviewers. This publication has emanated from research conducted with the financial support of Science Foundation Ireland under Grant Number SFI/12/RC/2289.

## References

Steven Bird, Robert Dale, Bonnie Dorr, Bryan Gibson, Mark Joseph, Min-Yen Kan, Dongwon Lee, Brett Powley, Dragomir Radev, and Yee Fan Tan. 2008. The ACL anthology reference corpus: a reference dataset for bibliographic research in computational linguistics. In *LREC'08*. Marrakech, Morocco.

Stefan Evert. 2004. *The Statistics of Word Cooccurrences Word Pairs and Collocations*. Ph.D. thesis, Institut für maschinelle Sprachverarbeitung, Universität Stuttgart.

KaterinaT. Frantzi, Sophia Ananiadou, and Junichi Tsujii. 1998. The $c$-value/$nc$-value method of automatic recognition for multi-word terms. In *Research and Advanced Technology for Digital Libraries*, volume 1513 of *LNCS*, pages 585–604.

Zellig S. Harris. 1954. Distributional structure. *Word, The Journal of the International Linguistic Association*, 10:146–162.

Kyo Kageura and Bin Umino. 1996. Methods of automatic term recognition: A review. *Terminology*, 3.2 (1996):259–289.

Pentti Kanerva, Jan Kristoferson, and Anders Holst. 2000. Random indexing of text samples for latent semantic analysis. In *Proceedings of the 22nd Annual Conference of the Cognitive Science Society*, pages 103–6. Erlbaum.

Alessandro Lenci. 2008. Distributional semantics in linguistic and cognitive research. *From context to meaning: Distributional models of the lexicon in linguistics and cognitive science, special issue of the Italian Journal of Linguistics*, 20/1:1–31.

Ping Li, Trevor J. Hastie, and Kenneth W. Church. 2006. Very sparse random projections. In *Proceedings of the 12th ACM SIGKDD International Conference on Knowledge Discovery and Data Mining*, KDD '06, pages 287–296. ACM, NY, USA.

Minh-Thang Luong, Thuy Dung Nguyen, and Min-Yen Kan. 2010. Logical structure recovery in scholarly articles with rich document features. *IJDLS*, 1(4):1–23.

Nils C. Newman, Alan L. Porter, David Newman, Cherie Courseault Trumbach, and Stephanie D. Bolan. 2014. Comparing methods to extract technical content for technological intelligence. *JET-M*, 32(0):97 – 109.

Behrang QasemiZadeh. 2010. Towards technology structure mining from text by linguistics analysis. DERI technical report, National University of Ireland, Galway.

Magnus Sahlgren. 2008. The distributional hypothesis. *Italian Journal of Linguistics*, 20:33–54.

Magnus Sahlgren, Anders Holst, and Pentti Kanerva. 2008. Permutations as a means to encode order in word space. In V. Sloutsky, B. Love, and K. Mcrae, editors, *Proceedings of the 30th Annual Conference of the Cognitive Science Society*, pages 1300–1305. Cognitive Science Society, Austin, TX.

Peter D. Turney and Patrick Pantel. 2010. From frequency to meaning: vector space models of semantics. *J. Artif. Int. Res.*, 37(1):141–188.

Yiming Yang. 1999. An evaluation of statistical approaches to text categorization. *Inf. Retr.*, 1(1-2):69–90.

Behrang Q. Zadeh and Siegfried Handschuh. 2014a. The ACL RD-TEC: a dataset for benchmarking terminology extraction and classification in computational linguistics. In *Coling 2014 CompuTerm 2014*. Dublin, Ireland.

Behrang Q. Zadeh and Siegfried Handschuh. 2014b. Evaluation of technology term recognition with random indexing. In *LREC'14*. European Language Resources Association (ELRA), Reykjavik, Iceland.

Behrang Q. Zadeh and Siegfried Handschuh. 2014c. Random manhattan indexing. *Database and Expert Systems Applications (DEXA), 25th International Workshop on*. IEEE, Munich, Germany.

# Jargon-Term Extraction by Chunking

**Adam Meyers**[†]**, Zachary Glass**[†]**, Angus Grieve-Smith**[†]**, Yifan He**[†]**,**
**Shasha Liao**[‡] **and Ralph Grishman**[†]
New York University[†], Google[‡]
meyers/angus/yhe/grishman@cs.nyu.edu, zglass@alumni.princeton.edu

**Abstract**

NLP definitions of *Terminology* are usually application-dependent. IR terms are noun sequences that characterize topics. Terms can also be arguments for relations like abbreviation, definition or IS-A. In contrast, this paper explores techniques for extracting terms fitting a broader definition: noun sequences specific to topics and not well-known to naive adults. We describe a chunking-based approach, an evaluation, and applications to non-topic-specific relation extraction.

## 1 Introduction

Webster's II New College Dictionary (Houghton Mifflin Company, 2001, p.1138) defines terminology as: *The vocabulary of technical terms and usages appropriate to a particular field, subject, science, or art.* Systems for automatically extracting instances of terminology (terms) usually assume narrow operational definitions that are compatible with particular tasks. Terminology, in the context of Information Retrieval (IR) (Jacquemin and Bourigault, 2003) refers to keyword search terms (*microarray, potato, genetic algorithm*), single or multi-word (mostly nominal) expressions collectively representing topics of documents that contain them. These same terms are also used for creating domain-specific thesauri and ontologies (Velardi et al., 2001). We will refer to these types of terms as *topic-terms* and this type of terminology *topic-terminology*. In other work, types of terminology (genes, chemical names, biological processes, etc.) are defined relative to a specific field like Chemistry or Biology (Kim et al., 2003; Corbett et al., 2007; Bada et al., 2010). These classes are used for narrow tasks, e.g., Information Extraction (IE) slot filling tasks within a particular genre of interest (Giuliano et al., 2006; Bundschus et al., 2008; BioCreAtIvE, 2006). Other projects are limited to Information Extraction tasks that may not be terminology-specific, but have terms as arguments, e.g., (Schwartz and Hearst, 2003; Jin et al., 2013) detect abbreviation and definition relations respectively and the arguments are terms. In contrast to this previous work, we have built a system that extracts a larger set of terminology, which we call *jargon-terminology*. Jargon-terms may include *ultracentrifuge*, which is unlikely to be a topic-term of a current biology article, but will not include *potato*, a non-technical word that could be a valid topic-term. We aim to find all the jargon-terms found in a text, not just the ones that fill slots for specific relations. As we show, jargon-terminology closely matches the notional (e.g., Webster's) definition of terminology. Furthermore, the important nominals in technical documents tend to be jargon-terms, making them likely arguments of a wide variety of possible IE relations (concepts or objects that are invented, two nominals that are in contrast, one object that is "better than" another, etc.). Specifically, the identification of jargon-terms lays the ground for IE tasks that are not genre or task dependent. Our approach which finds all instances of terms (tokens) in text is conducive to these tasks. In contrast, topic-term detection techniques find smaller sets of terms (types), each term occurring multiple times and the set of terms collectively represents a topic, in a similar way that a set of documents can represent a topic.





*Proceedings of SADAATL 2014*, pages 11–20,
Dublin, Ireland, August 24, 2014.

This paper describes a system for extracting jargon-terms in technical documents (patents and journal articles); the evaluation of this system using manually annotated documents; and a set of information extraction (IE) relations which take jargon-terms as arguments. We incorporate previous work in terminology extraction, assuming that terminology is restricted to noun groups (minus some left modifiers) (Justeson and Katz, 1995); [1] and we use both topic-term extraction techniques (Navigli and Velardi, 2004) and relation-based extraction techniques (Jin et al., 2013) in components of our system. Rather than looking at the distribution of noun groups as a whole for determining term-hood, we refine the classes used by the noun group chunker itself, placing limitations on the candidate noun groups proposed and then filtering the output by setting thresholds on the number and quality of the "jargon-like" components of the phrase. The resulting system admits not only topic-terms, but also other non-topic instances of terminology. Using the more inclusive set of jargon-terms (rather than just topic-terms) as arguments of the IE relations in section 6, we are able to detect a larger and more informative set of relation. Furthermore, these relations are salient for a wide variety of genres (unlike those in (BioCreAtIvE, 2006)) – a genre-neutral definition of terminology makes this possible. For example, the CONTRAST relation between the two bold face terms in **necrotrophic effector system**$_{A1}$ *that is an exciting contrast to the* **biotrophic effector models**$_{A2}$. would be applicable in most academic genres. Our jargon-terms also contrast with the tactic of filling terminology slots in relations with any noun-group (Justeson and Katz, 1995), as such a strategy overgenerates, lowering precision.

## 2 Topic-term Extraction

Topic-term extractors (Velardi et al., 2001; Tomokiyo and Hurst, 2003) collect candidate terms (N-grams, noun groups, words) that are more representative of a foreground corpus (documents about a specific topic) than they are of a background corpus (documents about a wide range of topics), using statistical measures such as $\frac{Term\ Frequency}{Inverse\ Document\ Frequency}$ (TFIDF), or a variation thereof. Due to the metrics used and cutoffs assumed, the list of terms selected is usually no more than a few hundred distinct terms, even for a large set of foreground documents and tend to be especially salient to that topic. The terms can be phrases that lay people would not know (e.g., *microarray, genetic algorithm*) or common topics for that document set (e.g., *potato, computer*). Such systems rank all candidate terms, using cutoffs (minimum scores or percentages of the list) to separate out the highest-ranked terms as output. Thus sets of topic-terms, derived this way, are dependent on the foreground and background assumed, and the publication dates. So a precise definition would include such information, e.g., *topic-terms(biomedical-patents, random-patents, 1990–1999)* would refer to those topic-terms that differentiate a foreground of biomedical patents from the 1990s from a background of diverse patents from the same epoch. Narrower topics are possible (e.g., comparing DNA-microarray patents to the same background); or broader ones (e.g., if a diverse corpus including news articles, fiction and travel writing are the background set instead of patents, then patent terms such as *national stage application* may be highly ranked in the output). Thus topic-terms generated by these methods model a relationally based definition and are relative to the chosen foregrounds, backgrounds and dates.

Topic-terms can include words/phrases like *potato, wheat, rat, monkey*, which may be common subjects of some set of biomedical documents, but are not specific to a technical field. In contrast, jargon-terms would include words (like *ultracentrifuge, theorem, graduated cylinder*) that are specific to technical language, but don't tend to be topics of any current document of interest. Jargon-terms, like topic-terms, can be defined relative to a particular foreground (which can also be represented as a set of documents), but there is the implicit assumption that they all share the same background set: non-genre-specific language (or simply a very diverse set of documents). It is also possible to refer to terminology in general as the union of jargon-terms with respect to the set of specialized knowledge areas as foregrounds and all sharing the same background of non-genre-specific language. Jargon-terms, like topic-terms, are also time dependent, since some terms will eventually be absorbed into the common lexicon, e.g., *computer*. However, we can make the simplifying assumption that we are talking about jargon in the present

[1] We restrict our scope to nominal terminology, but acknowledge the importance of non-nominal terminology, e.g., event verb terms (*calcify, coactivate*) which are crucial to IE.

time. Furthermore, jargon-term status is somewhat less time sensitive than topic-term status because terminology is absorbed very sparingly (and very slowly) into the popular lexicon, whereas topics go in and out of fashion quickly within a literature that is meant for an expert audience. Ignoring the *potato* type cases, topic-terms are a proper subset of jargon-terms and, thus, the set of jargon-terms is larger than the set of topic-terms. Finally, topic terms are ranked with respect to how well they can serve as keywords, i.e., how specific they are to a particular document set, whereas +/-jargon-term is a binary distinction.

We built a topic term extractor that combines several metrics together in an ensemble including: TFIDF, KL Divergence (Cover and Thomas, 1991; Hisamitsu et al., 1999) and a combination of Domain Relevance and Document Consensus (DRDC) based on (Navigli and Velardi, 2004). Furthermore, we filtered the output by requiring that each term would be recognized as a term by the jargon-term chunker described below in section 3. We manually scored the top 100 terms generated for two classes of biology patents (US patent classes 435 and 436) and achieved accuracies of 85% and 76% respectively. We also manually evaluated the top 100 terms taken from biology articles, yielding an accuracy of about 88%. As discussed, we use the output of this system for our jargon-term extraction system.

## 3 Jargon-term Extraction by Chunking

(Justeson and Katz, 1995) uses manual rules to detect noun groups (sequences of nouns and adjectives ending in a noun) with the goal of detecting instances of topic-terms. They filter out those noun groups that occur only once in the document on the theory that the multiply used noun groups are more likely to be topics. They manually score their output from two computer science articles and one biotechnology article, with 146, 350 and 834 instances of terms and achieve accuracies of 96%, 86% and 77%. (Frantzi et al., 2000) uses linguistic rules similar to noun chunking to detect candidate terms; filters the results using a stop list and other linguistic constraints; uses statistical filters to determine whether substrings are likely to be terms as well; and uses statistical filters based on neighboring words (context). (Frantzi et al., 2000) ranks their terms by scores and achieve about 75% accuracy for the top 40 terms – their system is tested on medical records (quite a different corpus form ours). Our system identifies all instances of terminology (not just topic terms) and identifies many more instances per document (919, 1131 and 2166) than (Justeson and Katz, 1995) or (Frank, 2000). As we aim to find all instances of jargon-terms, we evaluate for both precision and recall rather than just accuracy (section 5). Two of the documents that we test on are patents, which have a very different word distribution than articles. In fact, due to both the amount of repetition in patents and the presence of multiple types of terminology (legal terms as well as topic-related terms), it is hard to imagine that eliminating terms occurring below a frequency threshold (as with (Justeson and Katz, 1995)) would be an effective method of filtering. Furthermore, (Frank, 2000) used a very different corpus than we did and they focused on a slightly different problem (e.g., we did not attempt to find the highest-ranked terms and we did not attempt to find both long terms and substrings which were terms). Thus while it is appropriate to compare our methodology, it is difficult to compare our results.

We have implemented a hand-crafted term extractor, which we will call a jargon-term chunker because it functions in much the same way as a noun group chunker. It uses a deterministic finite state machine, based on parts of speech (POS) and a fine-tuned set of lexical categories. We observed that jargon-terms are typically noun groups, minus some left modifiers, and normally include words that are not in standard vocabulary or belong to certain other classes of words (e.g., nominalizations). While topic-term techniques factor the distribution of whole term sequences into the choice of topic-terms, our method focuses on the distribution of words within topic-term sequences. The primary function of POS classification is to cluster words distributionally in a language. A POS tag reflects the syntactic distribution of the word in the sense that words with the same POS should be able to replace each other in sentences. Morphologically, POSs are subject to the same morphological variation (prefixes, suffixes, tense, gender, number, etc.). For example, the English word *duck* belongs to the POS *noun* because it tends to occur: after a determiner, after an adjective, and ending a unit that can be the subject of a verb: nouns are substitutable for each other. Furthermore, it has a plural form resulting from an -s or -es suffix, etc. Similarly, we hold that the presence of particular classes of words within a noun group affects its potential to function as a jargon-term. As will become evident, we can use topic-term-like metrics to identify some of these word classes. Furthermore, given our previous assertion that topic-terms are a subset of jargon-terms, we assume that the most saliently ranked topic-terms are also jargon-terms and words that are commonly parts of topic-terms tend to be parts of jargon-terms. There are also "morphological properties" that are indicative of subsets of jargon-terms: allCap acronyms, chemical formulas, etc.

Our system classifies each word using POS tags, manually created dictionaries and the output of our own topic-term system. These classifications are achieved in four stages. In the first stage we divide the text into smaller segments using coordinate conjunctions (*and*, *or*, *as well as*, ...) and punctuation (periods, left/right parentheses and brackets, quotation marks, commas, colons, semi-colons). These segments are typically smaller than the level of the sentence, but larger than most noun groups. These segments are good units to process because they are larger than jargon-terms (substrings of noun groups) and smaller than sentences (and thus provide a smaller search space). In the second stage, potential jargon-term (PJs) are generated by processing tokens from left to right and classifying them using a finite state machine (FSM). The third stage filters the PJs generated with a set of manually constructed constraints, yielding a set of jargon-terms. A final filter (stage 4) identifies named entities and separates them out from the true jargon-terms: it turns out that many named entities have similar phrase-internal properties as jargon-terms.

The FSM (that generates PJs) in the second stage includes the following states (Ramshaw and Marcus, 1995): START (S) (marking the beginning of a segment), Begin Term (B-T), Inside Term (I-T), End Term (E-T), and Other (O). A PJ is a sequence consisting of: (a) a single E-T; or (b) exactly one B-T, followed by zero or more instances of I-T, followed by zero or one instances of E-T. Each transition to a new state is conditioned on: (a) the (extended) POS tag of the current word; (b) the extended POS tag of the previous word; and (c) the previous state. The extended POSs are derived from the output of a Penn-Treebank-based POS tagger and refinements based on machine readable dictionaries, including COMLEX Syntax (Macleod et al., 1997), NOMLEX (Macleod et al., 1998), and some manually encoded dictionaries created for this project. Table 1 describes the transitions in the FSM (unspecified entries mean no restriction). ELSE indicates that in all cases other than those listed, the FST goes to state O. Extended POS tags are classified as follows.

**Adjectives**, words with POS tags JJ, JJR or JJS, are subdivided into:

**STAT-ADJ:** Words in this class are marked adjective in our POS dictionaries and found as the first word in one of the top ranked topic-terms (for the topic associated with the input document).

**TECH-ADJ:** If an adjective ends in a suffix indicating (*-ic*, *-cous*, *-xous*, and several others) it is a technical word, but it is not found in our list of exceptions, it is marked TECH-ADJ.

**NAT-ADJ:** An adjective, usually capitalized, that is the adjectival form of a country, state, city or continent, e.g., *European*, *Indian*, *Peruvian*, ...

**CAP-ADJ:** An adjective such that the first letter is capitalized (but is not marked NAT-ADJ).

**ADJ:** Other adjectives

**Nouns** are marked NN or NNS by the POS tagger and are the default POS for out of vocabulary (OOV) words. POS tags like NNP, NNPS and FW (proper nouns and foreign nouns) are not reliable for our POS tagger (trained on news) when applied to patents and technical articles. So NOUN is also assumed for these. Subclasses include:

**O-NOUN:** (Singular or plural) nouns not found in any of our dictionaries (COMLEX plus some person names) or nouns found in lists of specialized vocabulary which currently include chemical names.

**PER-NOUN:** Nouns beginning with a capital that are in our dictionary of first and last names.

**PLUR-NOUN:** Nouns with POS NNS nouns that are not marked O-NOUN or PER-NOUN.

**C-NOUN:** Nouns with POS NN that are not marked O-NOUN or PER-NOUN.

**Verbs** Only **ING-VERB**s (VBG) and **ED-VERB**s (VBN and VBD) are needed for this task (other verbs trigger state O). Finally, we use the following additional POS tags:

**POSS:** POS for *'s*, split off from a possessive noun.

**PREP:** All prepositions (POS IN and TO)

**ROM-NUM:** Roman numerals (I, II, ..., MMM)

| Previous POS | Current POS | Previous State | New State |
|---|---|---|---|
| | DET, PREP, POSS, VERB | | O |
| O-NOUN, C-NOUN, PLUR-NOUN | ROM-NUM | B-T, I-T | E-T |
| | PLUR-NOUN | B-T,I-T | I-T |
| | ADJ, CAP-ADJ | I-T | I-T |
| | C-NOUN, PER-NOUN, O-NOUN | B-T, I-T | I-T |
| O-NOUN | CAP-ADJ, TECH-ADJ, STAT-ADJ, NAT-ADJ | B-T, I-T | I-T |
| | CAP-ADJ, TECH-ADJ, NAT-ADJ, ING-VERB, ED-VERB, STAT-ADJ C-NOUN, O-NOUN, PER-NOUN | E-T, O, S | B-T |
| TECH-ADJ, NAT-ADJ ADJ, CAP-ADJ | TECH-ADJ, NAT-ADJ ADJ, CAP-ADJ | B-T, I-T | I-T |
| ELSE | | | O |

Table 1: Transition Table

A potential jargon-term (PJ) is an actual jargon-term unless it is filtered out as follows. First, a jargon term $J$ must meet all of these conditions:

1. $J$ must contain at least one noun.
2. $J$ must be more than one character long, not counting a final period.
3. $J$ must contain at least one word consisting completely of alphabetic characters.
4. $J$ must not end in a common abbreviation from a list (e.g., cf., etc.)
5. $J$ must not contain a word that violates a morphological filter, designed to rule out numeric identifiers (patent numbers), mathematical formulas and other non-words. This rules out tokens beginning with numbers that include letters; tokens including plus signs, ampersands, subscripts, superscripts; tokens containing no alphanumeric characters at all, etc.
6. $J$ must not contain a word that is a member of a list of common patent section headings.

Secondly, a jargon-term $J$ must satisfy at least one of the following additional conditions:

1. $J$ = highly ranked topic-term or a substring of $J$ is a highly ranked topic-term.
2. $J$ contains at least one O-NOUN.
3. $J$ consists of at least 4 words, at least 3 of which are either nominalizations (C-NOUNs found in NOMLEX-PLUS (Meyers et al., 2004; Meyers, 2007)) or TECH-ADJs.
4. $J$ = nominalization at least 11 characters long.
5. $J$ = multi-word ending in a common noun and containing a nominalization.

A final stage aims to distinguish named entities from jargon-terms. It turns out that named entities, like jargon terms, include many out of vocabulary words. Thus we look for NEs among those PJs that remain after stage 3 and contain capitalized words (a single capital letter followed by lowercase letters). These NE filters are based on manually collected lists of named entities and nationality adjectives, as well as common NE endings. Dictionary lookup is used to assign GPE (ACE's Geopolitical Entity) to *New York* or *American*; LOC(ation) to *Aegean Sea* and *Ural Mountains*; and FAC(ility) to *Panama Canal* and *Suez Canal*. Plurals of nationality words, e.g., *Americans* are filtered out as non-terms. PJs are filtered by endings typically associated with non-terms, e.g., *et al* signals PJs as citations to articles and honorifics (Esq, PhD, Jr, Snr) signal PER(son) named entities. Finally, if at least one of the words in a multi-word term is a first or last person name, we can further filter them by endings, where ORGanization endings include *Agency, Association, College* and more than 65 others; GPE endings include *Heights, Township, Park*; LOC(ation) endings include *Street, Avenue* and *Boulevard.* It turns out that 2 word capitalized structures including at least one person name are usually either ORG or GPE in our patent corpus, and we maintain this ambiguity, but mark them as non-terms.

We have described a first implementation of a jargon-term chunker based on a combination of principles previously implemented in noun group chunking and topic-term extraction systems. The chunker can use essentially the same algorithms as previous noun group chunkers, though in this case we used a manual-rule based FSM. The extended POSs are defined according to conventional POS (representing substitutability, morphology, etc.), statistical topic-term extraction, OOV status (absence from our dictionary) or presence in specialized dictionaries (NOMLEX, dictionary of chemicals, etc.). We use topic-term extraction to identify both particular noun sequences (high-ranked topic-terms) and some of their components (STAT-ADJ), and could extend this strategy to other components, e.g., common head nouns. We approximated the concept of "rare word" by noting which words were not found in our standard dictionary (O-NOUN). As is well-known, "noun" and "adjective" are the first and second most frequent POS for OOV words and both POSs are typically found as part of noun groups. Furthermore, rare instances of O-NOUN (and OOV adjectives) are typically parts of jargon-terms. This approximation is fine-tuned by the addition of word lists (e.g., chemicals). In future work, we can use more distributional information to fine-tune these categories, e.g., we can use topic-term techniques to identify single topic words (nouns and adjectives) and experiment with these additional POS (instead of or in addition to the current POS classes).

## 4 The Annotator Definition of Jargon-Term

For purposes of annotation, we defined *jargon-term* as a word or multi-word nominal expression that is specific to some technical sublanguage. It need not be a proper noun, but it should be conventionalized in one of the following two ways:

1. The term is defined early (possibly by being abbreviated) in the document and used repeatedly (possibly only in its abbreviated form).
2. The term is special to a particular field or subfield (not necessarily the field of the document being annotated). It is not enough if the document contains a useful description of an object of interest – there must be some conventional, definable term that can be used and reused. Thus multi-word expressions that are defined as jargon terms must be somewhat word-like – mere descriptions that are never reused verbatim are not jargon terms. (Justeson and Katz, 1995) goes further than we do: they require that terms be reused within the document being annotated, whereas we only require that they be reused (e.g., frequent hits in a web search).

Criterion 2 leaves open the question of how specific to a genre an expression must be to be considered a jargon-term. At an intuitive level, we would like to exclude words like *patient*, which occur frequently in medical texts, but are also commonly found in non-expert, everyday language. By contrast, we would like to include words like *tumor* and *chromosome*, which are more intrinsic to technical language insofar as they have specialized definitions and subtypes within medical language. To clarify, we posited that a jargon-term must be sufficiently specialized so that a *typical naive adult* should not be expected to know the meaning of the term. We developed 2 alternative models of a naive adult:

1. *Homer Simpson*, an animated TV character who caricatures the typical naive adult–the annotators invoke the question: *Would Homer Simpson know what this means?*
2. **The Juvenile Fiction sub-corpus of the COCA:** The annotators go to `http://corpus.byu.edu/coca/` and search under FIC:Juvenile – a single occurrence of an expression in this corpus suggests that it is probably not a jargon-term.

In addition, several rules limited the span of terms to include the head and left modifiers that collocate with the heads. Decisions about which modifiers to include in a term were difficult. However, as this

| | Doc | Terms | Strict Matches | Strict Pre | Strict Rec | Strict F | Sloppy Matches | Sloppy Pre | Sloppy Rec | Sloppy F |
|---|---|---|---|---|---|---|---|---|---|---|
| **Annot 1** | SRP | 1131 | 798 | 70.8% | 70.6% | 70.7% | 1041 | 92.5% | 92.0% | 92.2% |
| | SUP | 2166 | 1809 | 87.5% | 83.5% | 85.5% | 1992 | 96.3% | 92.0% | 94.1% |
| | VVA | 919 | 713 | 90.9% | 77.6% | 83.7% | 762 | 97.2% | 82.9% | 89.5% |
| **Annot 2** | SRP | 1131 | 960 | 98.4% | 84.9% | 91.1% | 968 | 99.2% | 85.6% | 91.9% |
| | SUP | 2166 | 1999 | 95.5% | 92.3% | 93.8% | 2062 | 98.5% | 95.2% | 96.8% |
| | VVA | 919 | 838 | 97.4% | 91.2% | 94.2% | 855 | 99.4% | 93.0% | 96.1% |
| **Base 1** | SRP | 1131 | 602 | 24.3% | 53.2% | 33.4% | 968 | 44.2% | 96.8% | 60.7% |
| | SUP | 2166 | 1367 | 36.5% | 63.1% | 46.2% | 1897 | 50.6% | 87.6% | 64.2% |
| | VVA | 919 | 576 | 28.5% | 62.7% | 39.2% | 887 | 44.0% | 96.5% | 60.4% |
| **Base 2:** | SRP | 1131 | 66 | 24.9% | 5.8% | 9.5% | 151 | 57.0% | 13.4% | 21.6% |
| | SUP | 2166 | 771 | 52.3% | 35.6% | 42.4% | 1007 | 68.4% | 46.5% | 55.3% |
| | VVA | 919 | 270 | 45.8% | 29.4% | 35.8% | 392 | 66.5% | 42.6% | 51.9% |
| **System Without Filter** | SRP | 1131 | 932 | 39.0% | 82.4% | 53.0% | 1121 | 46.9% | 99.1% | 63.7% |
| | SUP | 2166 | 1475 | 39.7% | 68.1% | 50.2% | 1962 | 52.8% | 90.6% | 66.7% |
| | VVA | 919 | 629 | 27.8% | 68.4% | 39.5% | 900 | 39.8% | 97.9% | 56.6% |
| **System** | SRP | 1131 | 669 | 69.0% | 59.2% | 63.7% | 802 | 82.8% | 70.9% | 76.4% |
| | SUP | 2166 | 1193 | 64.7% | 55.1% | 59.5% | 1526 | 82.8% | 70.5% | 76.1% |
| | VVA | 919 | 581 | 62.1% | 63.2% | 62.7% | 722 | 77.2% | 78.6% | 77.9% |

Table 2: Evaluation of Annotation, Baseline and Complete System Against Adjudicated Data

evaluation task came on the heels of the relation extraction task described in section 6, we based our extent rules on the definitions and the set of problematic examples that were discussed and cataloged during that project. This essentially formed the annotation equivalent of case-law for extents. We will make our annotation specifications available on-line, along with discussions of these cases.

## 5 Evaluation

For evaluation purposes, we annotated all the instances of jargon-terms in a speech recognition patent (SRP), a sunscreen patent (SUP) and an article about a virus vaccine (VVA). Each document was annotated by 2 people and then adjudicated by Annotator 2 after discussing controversial cases. Table 2 scores the system, annotator 1 and annotator 2, by comparing each against the answer key providing: number of terms in the answer key, number of matches, precision, recall and F-measure. The "strict" scores are based on exact matches between system terms and answer key terms, whereas the "sloppy" scores count as correct instances where part of a system term matches part of an answer key term (span errors). As the SRP document was annotated first, some of specification agreement process took place after annotation and the scores for annotators are somewhat lower than for the other documents. However, Annotator 1's scores for SUP and VVA are good approximations of how well a human being should be expected to perform and the system's scores should be compared to Annotator 1 (i.e., accounting for the adjudicator's bias).

There are 4 system results: two baseline systems and two stages of the system described in section 3. Baseline 1 assumes terms derived by removing determiners from noun groups – we used an MEMM chunker using features from the GENIA corpus (Kim et al., 2003). That system has relatively high recall, but overgenerates, yielding a lower precision and F-measure than our full system – it is also inaccurate at determining the extent of terms. Baseline 2 restricts the noun groups from this same chunker to those with O-NOUN heads. This improves the precision at a high cost to recall. Similarly, we first ran our system without filtering the potential jargon-terms, and then we ran the full system. Clearly our more complex strategy performs better than these baselines and the linguistic filters increase precision more than they reduce recall, resulting in higher F-measures (though low-precision high-recall output may be better for some applications).

## 6 Relations with Jargon-Terms

(Meyers et al., 2014) describes the annotation of 200 PubMed articles from and 26 patents with several relations, as well as a system for automatically extracting relations. It turned out that the automatic system depended on the creation of a jargon-term extraction system and thus that work was the major motivating factor for the research described here. Choosing topic-terms as potential arguments would have resulted in low recall. In contrast, allowing any noun-group to be an argument would have lowered precision, e.g., *diagram*, *large number*, *accordance* and *first step* are unlikely to be valid arguments of relations. In the example: *The resequencing* **pathogen microarray**$_{A2}$ *in the diagram is a promising new technology.*, we can detect that the authors of the articles view *pathogen microarray* as significant, and not the NG *diagram*. By selecting jargon-terms as potential arguments we are selecting the most probable noun group arguments for our relations. For the current system (which does not use a parser), the system performs best if non-jargon-terms are not considered as potential relation arguments at all. However, one could imagine a wider coverage (and slower) system incorporating a preference for jargon-terms (like a selection restriction) with dependency-based constraints.

We will only describe a few of these relations due to space considerations. Our relations include: (1) **ABBREVIATE**, a relation between two terms that are equivalent. In the normal case, one term is clearly a shorthand version of the other, e.g., "The **D. melanogaster gene Muscle LIM protein at 84B**$_{A1}$ (abbreviated as **Mlp84B**$_{A2}$)". However, in the special case (**ABBREVIATE:ALIAS**) neither term is a shorthand for the other. For example in "**Silver behenate**$_{A1}$, also known as **CH3-(CH2)20-COOAg**$_{A2}$", the chemical name establishes that this substance is a salt, whereas the formula provides the proportions of all its constituent elements; (2) **ORIGINATE**, the relation between an ARG1 (person, organization or document) and an ARG2 (a term), such that the ARG1 is an inventor, discoverer, manufacturer, or distributor of the ARG2 and some of these roles are differentiated as subtypes of the relation. Examples include the following: "**Eagle**$_{A1}$**'s minimum essential media**$_{A2}$ and **DOPG**$_{A2}$ was obtained from **Avanti Polar Lipids**$_{A1}$". (3) **EXEMPLIFY**, an IS-A relation (Hearst, 1992) between terms so that ARG1 is an instance of ARG2, e.g., "**Cytokines**$_{A2}$, for instance **interferon**$_{A1}$"; and "**proteins**$_{A2}$ such as **insulin**$_{A1}$"; (4) **CONTRAST** relations, e.g., "**necrotrophic effector system**$_{A1}$ that is an exciting contrast to the **biotrophic effector models**$_{A2}$"; (5) **BETTER_THAN** relations, e.g., "**Bayesian networks**$_{A1}$ hold a considerable advantage over **pairwise association tests**$_{A2}$"; and (6) **SIGNIFICANT** relations, e.g., "**Anaerobic SBs**$_{A2}$ are an emerging area of research and development" (ARG1, the author of the article, is implicit). These relations are applicable to most technical genres.

## 7 Concluding Remarks

We have described a method for extracting instances of jargon-terms with an F-measure of between 62% and 77% (strict vs sloppy), about 73% to 84% of human performance. We expect this work to facilitate the extraction of a wide reange of relations from technical documents. Previous work has focused on generating topic-terminology or term types, extracted over sets of documents. In contrast, we describe an effective method of extracting term tokens, which represent a larger percent of the instances of terminology in documents and constitute arguments of many more potential relations. Our work on relation extraction yielded very low recalls until we adopted this methodology. Consequently, we have obtained recall of over 50% for many relations (with precision ranging from 70% for OPINION relations like Significant to 96% for Originate.).

## Acknowledgments

Supported by the Intelligence Advanced Research Projects Activity (IARPA) via Department of Interior National Business Center contract number D11PC20154. The U.S. Government is authorized to reproduce and distribute reprints for Governmental purposes notwithstanding any copyright annotation thereon. Disclaimer: The views and conclusions contained herein are those of the authors and should not be interpreted as necessarily representing the official policies or endorsements, either expressed or implied, of IARPA, DoI/NBC, or the U.S. Government.

## References

M. Bada, L. E. Hunter, M. Eckert, and M. Palmer. 2010. An overview of the craft concept annotation guidelines. In *The Linguistic Annotation Workshop, ACL 2010*, pages 207–211.

BioCreAtIvE. 2006. Biocreative ii.

M. Bundschus, M. Dejori, M. Stetter, V Tresp, and H. Kriegel. 2008. Extraction of semantic biomedical relations from text using conditional random fields. *BMC Bioinformatics*, 9.

P. Corbett, C. Batchelor, and S. Teufel. 2007. Annotation of chemical named entities. In *BioNLP 2007*, pages 57–64.

Thomas M. Cover and Joy A. Thomas. 1991. *Elements of Information Theory*. Wiley-Interscience, New York.

A. Frank. 2000. Automatic F-Structure Annotation of Treebank Trees. In *Proceedings of The LFG00 Conference*, Berkeley.

K. Frantzi, S. Ananiadou, and H. Mima. 2000. Automatic recognition of multi-word terms:. the C-value/NC-value method. *International Journal on Digital Libraries*, 3(2):115–130.

C. Giuliano, A. Lavelli, and L. Romano. 2006. Exploiting shallow linguistic information for relation extraction from biomedical literature. In *EACL 2006*, pages 401–408, Trento.

M. Hearst. 1992. Automatic Acquisition of Hyponyms from Large Text Corpora. In *ACL 1992*, pages 539–545.

T. Hisamitsu, Y. Niwa, S. Nishioka, H. Sakurai, O. Imaichi, M. Iwayama, and A. Takano. 1999. Term extraction using a new measure of term representativeness. In *Proceedings of the First NTCIR Workshop on Research in Japanese Text Retrieval and Term Recognition*.

Houghton Mifflin Company. 2001. *Webster's II New College Dictionary*. Houghton Mifflin Company.

C. Jacquemin and D. Bourigault. 2003. Term Extraction and Automatic Indexing. In R. Mitkov, editor, *Handbook of Computational Linguistics*. Oxford University Press, Oxford.

Y. Jin, M. Kan, J. Ng, and X. He. 2013. Mining scientific terms and their definitions: A study of the acl anthology. In *EMNLP-2013*.

J. S. Justeson and S. M. Katz. 1995. Technical terminology: some linguistic properties and an algorithm for identification in text. *Natural Language Engineering*, 1(1):9–27.

J. D. Kim, T. Ohta, Y. Tateisi, and J. I. Tsujii. 2003. Genia corpus–a semantically annotated corpus for bio-textmining. *Bioinformatics*, 19 (suppl 1):i180–i182.

C. Macleod, R. Grishman, and A. Meyers. 1997. COMLEX Syntax. *Computers and the Humanities*, 31:459–481.

C. Macleod, R. Grishman, A. Meyers, L. Barrett, and R. Reeves. 1998. Nomlex: A lexicon of nominalizations. In *Proceedings of Euralex98*.

A. Meyers, R. Reeves, C. Macleod, R. Szekeley, V. Zielinska, and B. Young. 2004. The Cross-Breeding of Dictionaries. In *Proceedings of LREC-2004*, Lisbon, Portugal.

A. Meyers, G. Lee, A. Grieve-Smith, Y. He, and H. Taber. 2014. Annotating Relations in Scientific Articles. In *LREC-2014*.

A. Meyers. 2007. Those Other NomBank Dictionaries – Manual for Dictionaries that Come with NomBank. `http:nlp.cs.nyu.edu/meyers/nombank/nomdicts.pdf`.

R. Navigli and P. Velardi. 2004. Learning Domain Ontologies from Document Warehouses and Dedicated Web Sites. *Computational Linguistics*, 30.

L. A. Ramshaw and M. P. Marcus. 1995. Text Chunking using Transformation-Based Learning. In *ACL Third Workshop on Very Large Corpora*, pages 82–94.

A. Schwartz and M. Hearst. 2003. A simple algorithm for identifying abbreviation definitions in biomedical text. In *Pacific Composium on Biocomputing*.

T. Tomokiyo and M. Hurst. 2003. A language model approach to keyphrase extraction. In *ACL 2003 Workshop on Multiword Expressions: Analysis, Acquisition and Treatment*.

P. Velardi, M. Missikoff, and R. Basili. 2001. Identification of relevant terms to support the construction of domain ontologies. In *Workshop on Human Language Technology and Knowledge Management - Volume 2001*, pages 5:1–5:8.

# Ontology-based Technical Text Annotation

**François Lévy**[†] **Nadi Tomeh**[†] **Yue Ma**[‡]
{francois.levy,nadi.tomeh}@lipn.univ-paris13.fr[†], mayue@tcs.inf.tu-dresden.de[‡]
[†]Université Paris 13, Sorbonne Paris Cité, LIPN, Villetaneuse, France
[‡]Dresden University of Technology, Dresden, Germany

## Abstract

Powerful tools could help users explore and maintain domain specific documentations, provided that documents have been semantically annotated. For that, the annotations must be sufficiently specialized and rich, relying on some explicit semantic model, usually an ontology, that represents the semantics of the target domain. In this paper, we learn to annotate biomedical scientific publications with respect to a Gene Regulation Ontology. We devise a two-step approach to annotate semantic events and relations. The first step is recast as a text segmentation and labeling problem and solved using machine translation tools and a CRF, the second as multi-class classification. We evaluate the approach on the BioNLP-GRO benchmark, achieving an average 61% F-measure on the event detection by itself and 50% F-measure on biological relation annotation. This suggests that human annotators can be supported in domain specific semantic annotation tasks. Under different experimental settings, we also conclude some interesting observations: (1) For event detection and compared to classical time-consuming sequence labeling approach, the newly proposed machine translation based method performed equally well but with much less computation resource required. (2) A highly domain specific part of the task, namely proteins and transcription factors detection, is best performed by domain aware tools, which can be used separately as an initial step of the pipeline.

## 1 Introduction

As is mostly the case with technical documents, biomedical documents, a critical resource for many applications, are usually rich with domain knowledge. Efforts in formalizing biomedical information have resulted in many interesting biomedical ontologies, such as Gene Ontology and SNOMED CT. *Ontology-based semantic annotation* for biomedical documents is necessary to grasp important semantic information, to enhance interoperability among systems, and to allow for semantic search instead of plain text search (Welty and Ide, 1999; Uren et al., 2006; Nazarenko et al., 2011). Furthermore, it provides a platform for consistency checking, decisions support, etc.

Ideal annotation should be accurate, thus requiring intensive knowledge and context awareness, and it should be automatic at the same time, since expert work is time consuming. Many efforts have been made in this field, from named entity recognition (NER) to information extraction (Ciravegna et al., 2004; Kiryakov et al., 2004), both in open domain (Uren et al., 2006; Cucerzan, 2007; Mihalcea and Csomai, 2007) and particular domains (Wang, 2009; Liu et al., 2011). Most cases of NER or information extraction focus on a small set of categories to be annotated, such as *Person*, *Location*, *Organization*, *Misc*, etc. Such a scenario often requires a special vocabulary, and generally benefits much from a limited set of linguistic templates for names or verbs. These restrictions can be widened by linguistic efforts in recognizing relevant forms, but they are the condition of accuracy.

With the increasing importance of ontologies in general or in specific domains[1], annotating a text regarding to a rich ontology has become necessary. For example, the BioNLP ST'11 GENIA challenge



[1]For instance, the OBO site lists 130 biological ontologies. The NASA publishes SWEET, a set of 200 small ontologies dedicated to earth and environment. The ProtegeOntology Library lists around 90 items.



*Proceedings of SADAATL 2014*, pages 21–30,
Dublin, Ireland, August 24, 2014.

task involved merely 10 concepts and 6 relations, but BioNLP ST'13 GRO task concerns more than 200 concepts and 10 relations. Some ontology-based annotating systems exist and include SemTag (Dill et al., 2003), DBpediaSpotlight (Mendes et al., 2011), Wiki Machine (LiveMemories, 2010). However, each of them is devoted to a particular ontology, for instance, Stanford TAP entity catalog (Guha and McCool, 2003) for SemTag and DBpedia Lexicalization Dataset[2] for DBpediaSpotlight. Hence, these existing systems cannot be directly used to reliably annotate biomedical domain, which is the case of the present work. To this end, the challenge that we focus on is semantic annotation of texts in a particular technical domain with regards to a rather large ontology (a large set of categories), which comes with its technical language and involves uses of concepts or relations that are not named entities. In this kind of use cases, one can get some manual expert annotations, but generally not in large quantity. And one has to learn from them in order to annotate more. This paper experiments on a set of biological texts provided for the BioNLP GRO task[3]. Since our approach is solely data-driven, it can be directly applied to obtain helpful annotation on legal texts governing a particular activity, formalization of specifications and requirement engineering, conformance of permanent services to their defining contracts, etc.

The task at hand is described in section 2, together with the main features of the GRO ontology used in the experiments. We consider here a classical pipeline architecture. The subtasks are recast as machine translation and sequence labeling problems, and standard tools are used to solve them. The first layer is based on domain lexicons and is not our work. Our tools are applied to the detection of relations and events[4]. Section 3 presents experiments, results and comparisons on the annotation of event terms. Section 4 presents experiments in detecting relations and completing event terms with their arguments.

## 2 A Pipeline Approach to Ontology-Based Text Annotation

The GRO task (Kim et al., 2013) aims to populate the Gene Regulation Ontology (GRO) (Beisswanger et al., 2008) with events and relations identified from text. We consider here automatically annotating biomedical documents with respect to relations and events belonging to the GRO.

GRO has two top-level categories of concepts, Continuant and Occurrent, where the Occurrent branch has concepts for processes that are related to the regulation of gene expression (e.g. Transcription, RegulatoryProcess), and the Continuant branch has concepts mainly for physical entities that are involved in those processes (e.g. Gene, Protein, Cell). It also defines semantic relations (e.g. hasAgent, locatedIn) that link the instances of the concepts.

The representation involves three primary categories of annotation elements: entities (i.e. the instances of Continuant concepts), events (i.e. those of Occurrent concepts) and relations. Mentions of entities in text can be either contiguous or discontinuous spans that are assigned the most specific and appropriate Continuant concepts (e.g. TranscriptionFactor, CellularComponent). Event annotation is associated with the mention of a contiguous span in text (called event trigger) that explicitly suggests the annotated event type (e.g. "controls" - RegulatoryProcess). If a participant of an event, either an entity or another event, can be explicitly identified with a specific mention in text, the participant is annotated with its role in the event. In this task, only two types of roles are considered, hasAgent and hasPatient, where an agent of an event is an entity that causes or initiates the event (e.g. a protein that causes a regulation event), and a patient of an event is an entity on which the event is carried out (e.g. the gene that is expressed in a gene expression event) (Dowty, 1991). Relation annotation is to annotate other semantic relations (e.g. locatedIn, fromSpecies) between entities and/or events, i.e. those without event triggers. An example annotation is shown in Figure 1.

The annotation of Continuant concepts has been considered for a long time and has well established methods relying on large dictionaries. GRO task has provided these annotations and only evaluates events and relations detection, including the triggers of events. We produce the annotation in two steps. The first step takes as input a biological text and the corresponding Continuant concepts and produces Occurent concepts (event triggers and their types). We provide two different formalizations of this problem: one

[2] `http://dbpedia.org/Lexicalizations`

[3] accessible on http://2013.bionlp-st.org/tasks

[4] "Event" is taken here in a biological sense, which may not fit to the state-event-process distinction or other linguistic views

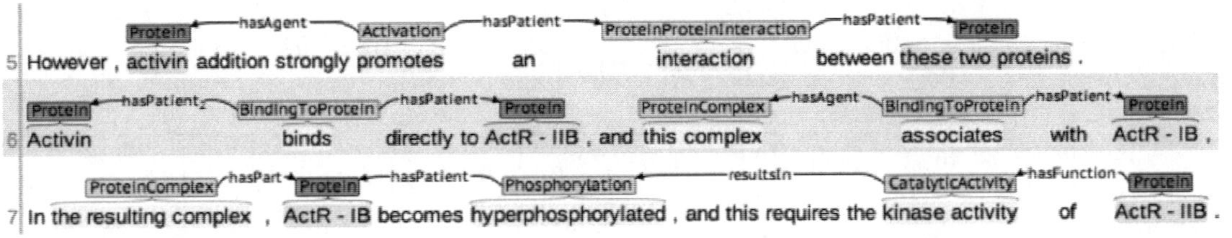


Figure 1: Example annotations from the GRO corpus (Kim et al., 2013).

as a named entity recognition problem, and the other as a machine translation problem. The second step takes as input the text and both Continuant and Occurrent concepts (predicted in step 1) and predicts relations between them. Relations are either: (a) an "event argument role" relation (hasAgent, hasPatient) between an Occurent concept and another concept, or (b) one of a small set of predefined relations between two concepts that do not involve trigger words (encodes, hasFunction, locatedIn, precedes, hasPart, resultsIn, fromSpecies, startsIn, endsIn)[5] We formalize this problem as a multi-class classification problem and solve it using a discriminative maximum-entropy classifier.

## 3 Step One: Event Annotation

In this step, event triggers (continuous span of text) are identified and given a label from the Occurrent concepts (98 label in total). We formalize this task as text segmentation and labeling, and compare two approaches to solve it: named-entity recognition approach and machine translation approach.

### 3.1 Event detection as named-entity recognition

A direct formalization of the event detection task is as named-entity recognition (hence named NER4SA). The NER task is to locate and classify elements of text into pre-defined categories. In our case, the elements are contiguous segments representing biological events, and the categories are their corresponding ontology-based occurrent labels. Conditional random fields (CRF), which represents the state of the art in sequence labeling, are widely used for NER (Finkel et al., 2005). This is mainly because they allow for discriminative training benefiting from manually annotated examples, and because of their ability to take the sequential structure into consideration through the flow of probabilistic information during inference. Here, the input sequence $\mathbf{x} = (x_1, ..., x_n)$ represents the words, and the output sequence $\mathbf{y} = (y_1, ..., y_n)$ represents the corresponding labels. The labels we use are the ontology-based Occurrent corresponding to events, combined with a segmentation marker in order to capture annotations possibly spanning multiple words. These markers are 'B' for beginning of event, 'I' for inside an event and 'O' for outside an event.

CRF is powerful in allowing for a wide range of features to be considered in the model. However, it rapidly becomes time and memory consuming when incorporating wide-range dependencies between labels. Therefore, in our experiment, we use a linear-chain CRF (bi-gram label dependency) with features including the current word as well as prefix and suffix character n-grams up to length 2. We compare two label schemes, one containing the 'B', 'I', and 'O' markers (called BIO) and a simpler 'I', and 'O' scheme (called IO).

Table 1 summarizes the results using the following settings: the training data and half of the development data from GRO task is taken to train CRF models, and the rest half development data is taken as test. We use the Stanford NER recognizer for the implementation [6]. The performance of the system varies significantly from an event trigger to another. For example, "GeneExpression" is well characterized and relatively easily detected as indicated by an F-measure of 88%, while "Disease" has a very bad recall resulting in a low F-measure of 21%. The majority of triggers such as "BindingToProtein" and "PositiveRegulation" lie in the middle. "RNASplicing" was not recognized at all, which is partially due to its

[5] Not all these relation types are present in the training and development data.

[6] http://nlp.stanford.edu/software/CRF-NER.shtml

| Trigger | Precision IO | Precision BIO | Recall IO | Recall BIO | F-measure IO | F-measure BIO | TP IO | TP BIO | FP IO | FP BIO | FN IO | FN BIO |
|---|---|---|---|---|---|---|---|---|---|---|---|---|
| BindingToProtein | 0.86 | | 0.60 | | 0.71 | | 18 | | 3 | | 12 | |
| Disease | 0,67 | | 0.13 | | 0.21 | | 2 | | 1 | | 14 | |
| GeneExpression | 0.85 | | 0.92 | | 0.88 | | 23 | | 4 | | 2 | |
| PositiveRegulation | 0.79 | | 0.61 | | 0.69 | | 30 | | 8 | | 19 | |
| RNASplicing | 0.00 | | 0.00 | | 0.00 | | 0 | | 1 | | 4 | |
| Localization | 0.00 | **0.50** | 0.00 | **0.13** | 0.00 | **0.20** | 0 | **1** | **1** | **1** | 8 | **7** |
| CellDeath | **1.00** | **1.00** | 0.33 | **0.67** | 0.50 | **0.80** | 1 | **2** | 0 | 0 | 2 | **1** |
| RegulatoryProcess | 0.69 | **0.75** | **0.39** | **0.39** | 0.50 | **0.51** | 9 | 9 | 4 | 3 | 14 | 14 |
| Aggregated | 0,76 | **0.77** | 0,43 | **0.44** | **0.556** | **0.563** | 136 | **138** | 42 | **41** | 175 | **173** |

Table 1: Event detection as NER results. TP is for true positive, FP for false positive, and FN for false negative.

small number of occurrences in the data. On the aggregated class of (all) event triggers, the best result is obtained using the BIO scheme: 56.3% F-measure with a precision of 77% but with a weaker recall (44%). However, as given in the first block of Table 1, in most of the case IO and BIO schemes resulted in a comparable performance for triggers such as "BindingToProtein" and "Disease". But there are three cases (second block of Table 1) where a more fine-grained representation BIO slightly outperformed the basic IO representation. These results suggest that the segmentation scheme is of little importance for the performance of NER4SA.

### 3.2 Event detection as phrase-based SMT

In this section, we model the semantic annotation of specialized documents as a phrase-based statistical machine translation task (hence named SMT4SA). This modeling provides a potential advantage compared to the CRF approach due to its capacity to recognize (possibly complex) phrases as the relevant textual units to translate (annotate for our task). However, it is more difficult to incorporate arbitrary features into the model. The simple idea in SMT4SA is to consider an initial unannotated text as if it was written in a "foreign" language, and the annotated text as the target "translated" text. Formally speaking, two sentences $\langle s_1, s_2 \rangle$ are given in two languages $L_1$ and $L_2$: $L_1$ is English and $L_2 = L_1 \cup Voc(O)$ is the union of English and the vocabulary of the ontology $Voc(O)$ used as semantic tagset.[7] We say that $s_2$ is an annotated version of $s_1$ if it is obtained by replacing some sequences of English words in $s_1$ by elements of $Voc(O)$ as shown in the following Table 2.

| | |
|---|---|
| Language $L_1$: | `The corresponding` **gene** `was assigned to` **chromosome 14q31**`, the same region where genetic alterations have been associated with several abnormalities of` **thyroid hormone response**. |
| Language $L_2$: | `The corresponding` **TTGene** `was assigned to` **TTChromosome**`, the same region where genetic alterations have been associated with several abnormalities of` **TTOrganicChemical TEResponseProcess**. |

Table 2: L1 and L2 languages (TT and TE escapes mark entities and events)

Several steps are performed in order to construct a phrase-based SMT (Koehn et al., 2003a). Word alignments are first computed from paired sentences, then phrase pairs are extracted such that no word inside the phrase pair is aligned to a word outside it; these extracted phrase pairs are stored in a phrase table with a set of features quantifying their quality. Such features include the conditional translation probability typically computed as normalized phrase frequencies in the corpus. One the system is trained, the translation process is carried out as a search for the best target sentence under a log-linear scoring function that combines several features. The scaling parameters of this function are tuned discrimina-

[7] To differentiate elements of $Voc(O)$ and the plain English vocabulary, names from $O$ are preceded by an escape character sequence in $Voc(O)$.

tively to optimize the translation performance on a small set of paired sentences. Given a sentence to be translated, it has to be segmented into phrases which are then individually translated, and last reordered to fit the typical order of the target language. Applied to semantic annotation, the translation relation is monotonic (i.e. involves no reordering) and many elements are identical to their translation. The training data we use provides one-to-one correspondence between the words and their label which allows us to compute exact word alignments between source and target sentences. The possibility to produce good annotations when plain lexical information is ambiguous relies on the learning algorithm and the projection of its results on the text, inasmuch it takes the context into account for disambiguation. Note also that the model accounts for tokens which must not be annotated (they are learned to be identically translated). SMT systems typically incorporate a language model (LM) which helps selecting the most probable annotated sentence from the large set of possibilities, and the phrase table functions as a sophisticated dictionary between the source and target languages. We use the KenLM language model Toolkit (Heafield et al., 2013) to train a language model for our experiments. To construct the phrase table we use the relatively simple but effective method defined in (Koehn et al., 2003b) but we use exact word alignment which we compute separately. The decoding is done by a beam search as implemented by Moses (Koehn et al., 2007). To localize the precise positions of semantic annotations predicted, we use the translation alignment between the two texts provided at the word level in the output of Moses. For example, giving "15-14 16-14" in the alignment for a sentence means that the 15th and 16th words in the original are replaced by the 14th word in the translated file. If the 14th word belongs to $Voc(O)$, such as $TTGene$, the concept $Gene$ is the semantic label associated to the 15th and 16th words of the original text.

### 3.2.1 Evaluation

We performed several experiments in order to discover which information helps obtaining the best accuracy. The input and output languages are called respectively L1 and L2, and varying these languages is the mean to focus on different subsets of the annotations. Due to the presence of Continuant annotations (c-annotations for short) in the input, the vocabulary of both L1 and L2 is extended beyond natural language in most experiments – this is more the case for L2 than it is for L1. 'Event trigger annotation' is henceforth abbreviated as et-annotation. For evaluation, two measures are used, one less requiring than the other: a positive annotation has either the same label and the same endpoints as a reference label (exact match), or at least one of these criteria is satisfied ('AL1 match'), provided that the positions, at least, intersect. The results are summarized in Table 3. In Table 3, 'expe1' is the main experiment, working exactly in the conditions proposed by the reference task: L1 has c-annotations and L2 has both c-and et-annotations. It can be compared to the aggregated results in table 1. Some variants have been made to separate the role of different factors. In 'expe2', L1 has no annotations at all and correspond to the raw input text, and L2 has everything, i.e., c- and et- ones. The expe2-a line gives a global result of evaluating the prediction of c- and et-annotations together: F-measures is 0.16 points below 'expe1', which is an important loss. However, computing the scores separately for the two kinds of annotation in the L2 language refines the view : the c-annotations (expe2-c line) are much worse than the et-ones (expe2-b line), which have only lost .03 points with respect to 'expe1'. From this, we conclude that c-annotations in L1 (as used in 'expe1') do not help much to learn et-annotations.

Analyzing the conditions of 'expe2', it can be seen that including the c-annotations from the references in L2 provide helpful information via the inverse probabilities used as a feature in the phrase table. So we made two more experiments to check each type of annotation by itself. In 'expe3', L1 is the unannotated text and L2 has only c-annotations. A slight improvement is observed on the F-measure of AL1 relative to 'expe2-c', while the exact case gets the same score. In fact, Moses suggests 20% more annotations but the ratio of true positive is worse. In 'expe4', L1 is the text and L2 has only et-annotations. The results are 0.02 points below 'expe1' and close to 'expe2-b', which proves that knowing c-annotations does not help us much to detect events triggers in this setting (note that c-annotations are used to detect events arguments in the next section). It also clearly shows that c-annotations are much harder to learn and that dictionaries or similar lexicon-based methods are more suitable.

The following experiments, namely 'exp5' and 'exp6' have no annotations in L1 compared to 'expe4'

| | #ref | #mo | #MP | #PG | #LG | #PLG | #AL1 | FPL | FAL1 |
|---|---|---|---|---|---|---|---|---|---|
| expe1 | 314 | 301 | 250 | 215 | 209 | 188 | 236 | 0.61 | 0.77 |
| expe2-a | 1229 | 869 | 734 | 520 | 594 | 476 | 638 | 0.45 | 0.61 |
| expe2-b | 313 | 328 | 248 | 210 | 214 | 190 | 234 | 0.59 | 0.73 |
| expe2-c | 916 | 541 | 468 | 310 | 391 | 286 | 415 | 0.39 | 0.57 |
| expe3 | 916 | 647 | 533 | 334 | 444 | 310 | 468 | 0.40 | 0.60 |
| expe4 | 313 | 329 | 253 | 217 | 213 | 191 | 239 | 0.60 | 0.74 |
| expe5 | 313 | 242 | 204 | 175 | 174 | 158 | 191 | 0.57 | 0.69 |
| expe6 | 313 | 306 | 246 | 210 | 204 | 181 | 233 | 0.58 | 0.75 |

The headers

| | | | |
|---|---|---|---|
| #ref | nbr of annotations in the reference | #PLG | nbr of exact (pos- and lab-good) matches |
| #mo | nbr of annotations in moses output | #AL1 | nbr of matches with at least one good attribute |
| #MP | nbr of matches (meeting pairs) | FPL | Fmesure - exact case |
| #PG | nbr of position-good matches | FAL1 | Fmesure - at least one case |
| #LG | nbr of label-good matches | | |

Table 3: The results of experiments on event detection as phrase-based SMT.

but only et-annotations in L2. In these experiments we use factored translation models (Koehn and Hoang, 2007) as implemented in Moses. Factors allow for incorporating supplementary information, in addition to the actual words, into the model. A simple analysis suggests that being an event term could be correlated to the nature of the word (favored by being a verb) or to the kind of dependency it enters in. We therefore added part-of-speech tags and grammatical dependency labels, computed from dependency trees, to L1. In 'expe5', the three L1 factors are compared altogether to L2 while in 'expe6' they are compared independently (and successively) to 'expe6'. In the first case, the performance drops by .03 to .06 points compared to 'expe4'. The second case has small effects on the two F-measures. Finally, using factor models in our settings does not improve the recognition of event terms.

To summarize, using c-annotations in L1, c- and et-annotations in L2 provides the best result, slightly better for et-annotations alone than if c-annotations are omitted. In these settings, et-annotation reaches a precision of 62% and a recall of 59% in the exact case (78% and 75% in the approximate one). We find 60% of exact positives; nearly 40% of the obtained annotations are not exact. Among these annotations, 15% captured at least one characteristic.

The predicted annotations obtained by both NER4SA and SMT4SA are then supplied to the next step in the pipeline. This second step in which relations and event arguments are computed is discussed in the next section.

## 4 Step Two: Relations and Event Arguments Annotation

In the second step of the pipeline, we take the output of the first step, namely the detected events, and we predict their arguments. We also predict other relations in the text.

The essential difference between the extraction of relations and that of event arguments is that relations link exactly two locations in the text while events link a variable number of locations and are supported by triggers. Nevertheless, we use a unified representation for both events and relations. A relation is a labeled link between two elements in the text. Examples of relation labels include '*locatedIn*' and '*fromSpecies*'. An event is a set of labeled relations between the event trigger (detected in step 1 of the pipeline) to an event argument which is another element of the text. Event-to-argument relations are labeled either '*hasAgent*' or '*hasPatient*'. Therefore, the problem of relation extractions boils down to a multi-class classification problem of candidate links. A candidate link involves two c- or et-annotations and is labeled by the biological relation name in the first case, or by an event argument role when its source is an event trigger. Note that the same event trigger may have several agent or patient roles.

### 4.1 A multi-class classification approach

For each candidate link between two elements of the text, we predict a label among 'none' (which indicate no link), '*hasAgent*', '*hasPatient*', '*locatedIn*', etc. Although we use the same representation for both event arguments annotation and relation annotation, we use two distinct multi-class classifier. The first classifier locate the arguments of each detected event and identify their roles. Event arguments can be Continuant concepts or other events. The second classifier extracts and label relations between any two concepts which can be Continuant or events. We perform these two tasks independently and combine their predictions afterward. For event arguments annotation: for each detected event, we assign one of the labels '*hasAgent*', '*hasPatient*', '*no-relation*' to all other entities. Similarly for relation annotation: for each pair of c- or et-annotations we predict a label which is either the label of the binary relation or the special label 'no-relation'. We use an implementation of a maximum-entropy classifier called Wapiti[8] (Lavergne et al., 2010). The set of features we used contains lexical and morpho-syntactic features extracted from the pair of entities in question. This include their lexical identities as they appear in the document as well as the ontology labels assigned to them. We also include the part-of-speech tags of involved words. Additionally, we include positional features such as the distance between the words in the document, computed as the number of words separating them, as well as their relative positions indicating which word precedes the other in the text. Furthermore, we use compound features resulting from combining pairs of the individual features.

### 4.2 Evaluation

The reference result has much more 'No' than 'Yes', and labeling randomly while respecting the proportion would give a good score for the No. So in the evaluation the numbers of true positives, false positives and false negatives only account for 'Yes' answers. The criterion is an exact match (label and position) at each end of the link. Table 4 gives the results for the relations appearing in our test set. The number of occurrences of each relation in the reference is pointed out. Except for the sparse '*hasFunction*', the precision is at least 57% and higher for relations which have the greatest number of occurrences. For recall, however, only '*fromSpecies*' relation has an important recall.The mean precision is 80% and the mean recall is 37%, which yields a F-measure of 50%.

| Relation | # of occurrences | Precision | Recall | F-measure |
|---|---|---|---|---|
| locatedIn | 182 | 0.73 | 0.26 | 0.38 |
| encodes | 46 | 0.57 | 0.21 | 0.31 |
| hasPart | 178 | 0.77 | 0.26 | 0.39 |
| fromSpecies | 172 | 0.90 | 0.69 | 0.78 |
| hasFunction | 24 | 0.20 | 0.08 | 0.12 |

Table 4: Detection of relations

The annotation of events presents seemingly more difficulties than relations: the precision is at best 60% for a much higher number of occurrences. The recall has the same order of magnitude for the agent role, and is better for the patient role which has twice more occurrences. The mean precision is 58%, and the mean recall is 36%. In the pipeline evaluation presented in the next section, errors due to event recognition will accumulate with errors proper to relation annotation.

| Class | # of occurrences | Precision | Recall | F-measure |
|---|---|---|---|---|
| hasPatient | 562 | 0.61 | 0.43 | 0.50 |
| hasAgent | 258 | 0.46 | 0.20 | 0.28 |

Table 5: Detecting arguments of events

[8] http://wapiti.limsi.fr

## 5 Pipeline Evaluation

The pipeline evaluation compares the relations and events obtained at the end of the pipeline to the reference. We have implemented the algorithm defined in the task description, and applied it to one unused half of the development data. In this evaluation, the data consist in 175 documents for training (of which 25 are reserved for Moses for tuning) and 25 for testing.

| | Events | | | Relations | | | Both | | |
|---|---|---|---|---|---|---|---|---|---|
| **Event detection** | Pr | Rc | F1 | Pr | Rc | F1 | Pr | Rc | F1 |
| NER4SA | .20 | .10 | .13 | .80 | .30 | .44 | .44 | .19 | .26 |
| SMT4SA | .14 | .13 | .13 | .80 | .30 | .44 | .32 | .21 | .25 |
| SMT4SA ∪ NER | .16 | .22 | .19 | .80 | .30 | .44 | .29 | .26 | .27 |

Table 6: Pipeline precision, recall and F-measure using strict matching for the NER4SA and SMT4SA approaches for event detection, and for their combination.

Relation detection has roughly the same figures as in table 4. The combination of event detection and arguments annotation obtains the same F-measure for both detection methods proposed, so the 5% point advantage of the second when tested out of the pipeline disappears here. Interestingly, using a combination (union) of the outputs of the NER and SMT approaches results in improvements in recall (and f1) over each approach in isolation.

## 6 Related work

Some effort has been dedicated to the recognition of ontology concepts in biomedical literature. This includes TextPresso (Muller et al., 2004) and GoPubMed (Doms and Schroeder, 2005). These approaches are based on term extraction methods to find the ontology concepts occurrences, together with some terminological variations. Systems like (Rebholz-Schuhmann et al., 2007) and FACTA (Tsuruoka et al., 2008) collect and display co-occurrences of ontology terms. However, they do not extract events and relations of the semantic types defined in ontologies. For event and relation extraction, (Klinger et al., 2011) use imperatively defined factor graphs to build Markov Networks that model inter-dependencies between mentions of events within sentences, and across sentence-boundaries. OSEE (jae Kim and Rebholz-Schuhmann, 2011) is a pattern matching system that learns language patterns for event extraction. Most similar to our work, is the TEES 2.1 system (Björne and Salakoski, 2013) which is based on multi-step SVM classifiers that learns event annotation by first locating triggers then identifying event arguments and finally selecting candidate events.

## 7 Conclusion

In this work, we have proposed a pipeline for annotating documents with domain sepcific ontologies and tested it on the BioNLP'13 GRO task. The two-step pipeline gives a flexible modeling choice, and is realized by different inner components. For the first step, the sequence labeling and phrase-based statistical machine translation approaches are applied. And we conducted detailed experiments to test different settings, from which we can conclude the following findings: (1) For the event recognition task, NER4SA, much computationally expensive due to its model complexity, did not result in higher scores than SMT4SA in terms of F-measure. It did give better precision, however at the expense of the recall. This shows that SMT4SA is a good practical modeling method for the task. (2) For SMT4SA, the extra features added by factored learning did not boost the system much, which means that a basic setting can capture the essential quality of the system. (3) For the relation detection based on the output of the pipeline, we obtained reasonable scores for events and relations. Interestingly, NER4SA, SMT4SA, or their combination did affect the detection of events, but not relations which is step-one independent. And the combination has had a better performance.

## Acknowledgements

We are thankful to the reviewers for their comments. This work is part of the program Investissements d'Avenir, overseen by the French National Research Agency, ANR-10-LABX-0083, (Labex EFL). We acknowledge financial support by the DFG Research Unit FOR 1513, project B1.

## References

[Beisswanger et al.2008] Elena Beisswanger, Vivian Lee, Jung jae Kim, Dietrich Rebholz-Schuhmann, Andrea Splendiani, Olivier Dameron, Stefan Schulz, and Udo Hahn. 2008. Gene regulation ontology (gro): Design principles and use cases. In *MIE*, volume 136 of *Studies in Health Technology and Informatics*, pages 9–14. IOS Press.

[Björne and Salakoski2013] Jari Björne and Tapio Salakoski. 2013. Tees 2.1: Automated annotation scheme learning in the bionlp 2013 shared task. In *Proceedings of the BioNLP Shared Task 2013 Workshop*, pages 16–25, Sofia, Bulgaria, August. Association for Computational Linguistics.

[Chiang2007] David Chiang. 2007. Hierarchical phrase-based translation. *Comput. Linguist.*, 33:201–228.

[Ciravegna et al.2004] Fabio Ciravegna, Sam Chapman, Alexiei Dingli, and Yorick Wilks. 2004. Learning to harvest information for the semantic web. In *Proceedings of ESWS'04*.

[Cucerzan2007] Silviu Cucerzan. 2007. Large-scale named entity disambiguation based on wikipedia data. In *Proceedings of EMNLP-CoNLL'07*, pages 708–716.

[Dill et al.2003] Stephen Dill, Nadav Eiron, David Gibson, Daniel Gruhl, R. Guha, Anant Jhingran, Tapas Kanungo, Sridhar Rajagopalan, Andrew Tomkins, John A. Tomlin, and Jason Y. Zien. 2003. Semtag and seeker: bootstrapping the semantic web via automated semantic annotation. In *Proceedings of WWW '03*, pages 178–186.

[Doms and Schroeder2005] Andreas Doms and Michael Schroeder. 2005. Gopubmed: exploring pubmed with the gene ontology. *Nucleic Acids Research*, 33(Web-Server-Issue):783–786.

[Dowty1991] David Dowty. 1991. Thematic proto-roles and argument selection. *Language*, 67:547–619.

[Finkel et al.2005] Jenny Rose Finkel, Trond Grenager, and Christopher Manning. 2005. Incorporating non-local information into information extraction systems by gibbs sampling. In *Proceedings of ACL'05*, pages 363–370.

[Guha and McCool2003] R Guha and R McCool. 2003. Tap: A semantic web test-bed. *Web Semantics Science Services and Agents on the World Wide Web*, 1(1):81–87.

[Heafield et al.2013] Kenneth Heafield, Ivan Pouzyrevsky, Jonathan H. Clark, and Philipp Koehn. 2013. Scalable modified Kneser-Ney language model estimation. In *Proceedings of the 51st Annual Meeting of the Association for Computational Linguistics*, pages 690–696, Sofia, Bulgaria, August.

[jae Kim and Rebholz-Schuhmann2011] Jung jae Kim and Dietrich Rebholz-Schuhmann. 2011. Improving the extraction of complex regulatory events from scientific text by using ontology-based inference. *J. Biomedical Semantics*, 2(S-5):S3.

[Kim et al.2013] Jung-Jae Kim, Xu Han, Vivian Lee, and Dietrich Rebholz-Schuhmann. 2013. Gro task: Populating the gene regulation ontology with events and relations. In *Proceedings of the BioNLP Shared Task 2013 Workshop*, pages 50–57, Sofia, Bulgaria, August. Association for Computational Linguistics.

[Kiryakov et al.2004] Atanas Kiryakov, Borislav Popov, Ivan Terziev, Dimitar Manov, and Damyan Ognyanoff. 2004. Semantic annotation, indexing, and retrieval. *Journal of Web Semantics*, 2:49–79.

[Klinger et al.2011] Roman Klinger, Sebastian Riedel, and Andrew McCallum. 2011. Inter-event dependencies support event extraction from biomedical literature. Mining Complex Entities from Network and Biomedical Data (MIND), European Conference on Machine Learning and Principles and Practice of Knowledge Discovery in Databases (ECML PKDD).

[Koehn and Hoang2007] Philipp Koehn and Hieu Hoang. 2007. Factored translation models. In *EMNLP-CoNLL*, pages 868–876. ACL.

[Koehn et al.2003a] Philipp Koehn, Franz Josef Och, and Daniel Marcu. 2003a. Statistical phrase-based translation. In *Proceedings of the 2003 Conference of the North American Chapter of the Association for Computational Linguistics on Human Language Technology - Volume 1*, NAACL '03, pages 48–54, Stroudsburg, PA, USA. Association for Computational Linguistics.

[Koehn et al.2003b] Philipp Koehn, Franz Josef Och, and Daniel Marcu. 2003b. Statistical phrase-based translation. In *HLT-NAACL*, pages 127–133.

[Koehn et al.2007] Philipp Koehn, Hieu Hoang, Alexandra Birch, Chris Callison-Burch, Marcello Federico, Nicola Bertoldi, Brooke Cowan, Wade Shen, Christine Moran, Richard Zens, Chris Dyer, Ondrej Bojar, Alexandra Constantin, and Evan Herbst. 2007. Moses: Open source toolkit for statistical machine translation. In *Proceedings of ACL'07*, pages 177–180.

[Lavergne et al.2010] Thomas Lavergne, Olivier Cappé, and François Yvon. 2010. Practical very large scale CRFs. In *Proceedings the 48th Annual Meeting of the Association for Computational Linguistics (ACL)*, pages 504–513. Association for Computational Linguistics, July.

[Liu et al.2011] Xiaohua Liu, Shaodian Zhang, Furu Wei, and Ming Zhou. 2011. Recognizing named entities in tweets. In *Proceedings of HLT '11*, pages 359–367.

[LiveMemories2010] LiveMemories. 2010. Livememories: Second year scientific report. Technical report, LiveMemories, December.

[Marcu and Wong2002] Daniel Marcu and William Wong. 2002. A phrase-based, joint probability model for statistical machine translation. In *Proceedings of EMNLP'02*, pages 133–139.

[Mendes et al.2011] Pablo N. Mendes, Max Jakob, Andrés García-Silva, and Christian Bizer. 2011. DBpedia Spotlight: Shedding light on the web of documents. In *Proceedings of I-Semantics'11*.

[Mihalcea and Csomai2007] Rada Mihalcea and Andras Csomai. 2007. Wikify!: linking documents to encyclopedic knowledge. In *Proceedings of CIKM'07*, pages 233–242.

[Muller et al.2004] H. Muller, E. Kenny, and P. Sternberg. 2004. Textpresso: An ontology-based information retrieval and extraction system for biological literature. *PLoS Biology*, 2(11):1984–1998.

[Nazarenko et al.2011] Adeline Nazarenko, Abdoulaye Guissé, Franois Lévy, Nouha Omrane, and Sylvie Szulman. 2011. Integrating written policies in business rule management systems. In *Proceedings of RuleML'11*.

[Och and Ney2003] Franz Josef Och and Hermann Ney. 2003. A systematic comparison of various statistical alignment models. *Computational Linguistics*, pages 19–51.

[Rebholz-Schuhmann et al.2007] Dietrich Rebholz-Schuhmann, Harald Kirsch, Miguel Arregui, Sylvain Gaudan, Mark Riethoven, and Peter Stoehr. 2007. Ebimed - text crunching to gather facts for proteins from medline. *Bioinformatics*, 23(2):237–244.

[Stolcke2002] Andreas Stolcke. 2002. Srilm — an extensible language modeling toolkit. In *In Proceedings of ICSLP'02*, pages 901–904.

[Tsuruoka et al.2008] Y Tsuruoka, J Tsujii, and S Ananiadou. 2008. Facta: a text search engine for finding associated biomedical concepts. *Bioinformatics*, 24(21):2559–2560, November.

[Uren et al.2006] Victoria S. Uren, Philipp Cimiano, José Iria, Siegfried Handschuh, Maria Vargas-Vera, Enrico Motta, and Fabio Ciravegna. 2006. Semantic annotation for knowledge management: Requirements and a survey of the state of the art. *J. Web Sem.*, 4(1):14–28.

[Wang2009] Yefeng Wang. 2009. Annotating and recognising named entities in clinical notes. In *ACL/AFNLP (Student Workshop)*, pages 18–26.

[Welty and Ide1999] Christopher Welty and Nancy Ide. 1999. Using the right tools: Enhancing retrieval from marked-up documents. In *Journal Computers and the Humanities*, pages 33–10.

# Extracting Aspects and Polarity from Patents

**Peter Anick, Marc Verhagen and James Pustejovsky**
Computer Science Department
Brandeis University
Waltham, MA, United States
Peter_anick@yahoo.com, marc@cs.brandeis.edu,
jamesp@cs.brandeis.edu

## Abstract

We describe an approach to terminology extraction from patent corpora that follows from a view of patents as "positive reviews" of inventions. As in aspect-based sentiment analysis, we focus on identifying not only the components of products but also the attributes and tasks which, in the case of patents, serve to justify an invention's utility. These semantic roles (component, task, attribute) can serve as a high level ontology for categorizing domain terminology, within which the positive/negative polarity of attributes serves to identify technical goals and obstacles. We show that bootstrapping using a very small set of domain-independent lexico-syntactic features may be sufficient for constructing domain-specific classifiers capable of assigning semantic roles and polarity to terms in domains as diverse as computer science and health.

## 1 Introduction

Automated data mining of patents has had a long history of research, driven by the large volume of patents produced each year and the many tasks to which they are put to use, including prior art investigation, competitive analysis, and trend detection and forecasting (Tseng, 2007). Much of this work has concentrated on bibliographic methods such as citation analysis, but text mining has also been widely explored as a way to assist analysts to characterize patents, discover relationships, and facilitate patent searches. One of the indicators of new technology emergence is the coinage, adoption and spread of new terms; hence the identification and tracking of technical terminology over time is of particular interest to researchers designing tools to support analysts engaged in technology forecasting (e.g., Woon, 2009; deMiranda, 2006)

For the most part, research into terminology extraction has either (1) focused on the identification of keywords within individual patents or corpora without regard to the roles played by the keywords within the text (e.g., Sheremetyeva, 2009) or, (2) engaged in fine-grained analysis of the semantics of narrow domains (e.g., Yang, 2008). In this paper we strive towards a middle ground, using a high-level classification suitable for all domains, inspired in part by recent work on sentiment analysis (Liu, 2012). In aspect-based sentiment analysis, natural language reviews of specific target entities, such as restaurants or cameras, are analyzed to extract *aspects,* i.e., features of the target entities, along with the sentiment expressed toward those features. In the restaurant domain, for example, aspects might include the breadth of the menu, quality of the service, preparation of the food, and cost. Aspects thus tend to capture the tasks that the entity is expected to perform and various dimensions and components related to those tasks. Sentiment reflects the reviewer's assessment of these aspects on a scale from negative to positive.

A patent application is required by definition to do three things: describe an invention, argue for its novelty, and justify its utility. The utility of a patent is typically defined by the accomplishment of a new task or an improvement to some existing task along one or more dimensions. Thus, a patent can be thought of as a *positive* review of a product with respect to specific aspects of its task(s). Indeed, the most commonly occurring verbs in patents include those indicative of *components* ("comprise", "include"), *attributes* ("increase", "reduce"), and *tasks* ("achieve", "perform"). Organizing keywords along these high-level distinctions, then, would allow patent analysts to explore terminological infor-





*Proceedings of SADAATL 2014*, pages 31–39,
Dublin, Ireland, August 24, 2014.

mation from several different relevant perspectives. Furthermore, given the interpretation of a patent as a positive review, it should be possible to identify the default polarity of measurable aspects in the context of a domain. For example, if a patent makes a reference to *increasing network bandwidth*, then this should lend support to the notion that network bandwidth is not only a relevant attribute within the patent's domain but also a positive one. Likewise, if a patent refers to *reducing power consumption*, then we might interpret power consumption as an aspect with negative polarity. For analysts trying to assess trends within a technology domain, tracking the occurrences of terms signifying tasks and attributes, along with their polarity, could help them characterize the changing goals and obstacles for inventors over time.

The US patent office receives over half a million patent applications a year.[1] These are classified by subject matter within several standardized hierarchical schemes, which permits dividing up the corpus of patents both by application date and subfield (e.g., computer science, health, chemistry). Since our goal is to support analysts across all domains, it is highly desirable to extract domain-specific aspects through semi-supervised machine learning rather than incur the cost of domain-specific knowledge engineering. To this end, we employed a bootstrapping approach in which a small number of domain independent features was used to generate a much larger number of domain dependent features for classification. We then applied naïve Bayes classification in a two-step classification process: first distinguishing attributes, components and tasks; and then classifying the extracted attribute terms by their polarity.

The paper is structured as follows. In section 2, we describe the system architecture. Section 3 shows results for two domains (computer science and health). In section 4, we present an evaluation of results and discuss issues and shortcomings of the current implementation. In section 5, we present related research and in section 6, our conclusions and directions for future work.

## 2 System architecture

### 2.1 Corpus processing

Our patent collection is a set of 7,101,711 US patents in XML-markup form from Lexis-Nexis. We divided the collection into subcorpora by application year and high-level domain using the patents' classification within the USPTO hierarchy. The XML markup was then used to extract the relevant portions of patents for further analysis. These sections included title, abstract, background, summary, description and claims. References, other than those embedded in the sections above, were omitted, as they contain many entity types (people, publications, and organizations) that are not particularly useful for our current task. The text of each section was extracted and broken into sentences by the Stanford tagger (Toutanova, 2003) which also tokenized and tagged each token with a part of speech tag.

We then chunked adjacent tokens into simple noun phrase chunks of the form (ADJECTIVE)? (NOUN)* NOUN.[2] We will hereafter refer to these chunks as *terms*. The majority of these patent terms fall into one of three major categories:

***Components***: the physical constituents or processes that make up an invention, as well as the objects impacted, produced by or used in the invention.

***Tasks***: the activities which inventions, their components or beneficiaries perform or undergo.

***Attributes***: the measureable dimensions of tasks and components mentioned in the patent.

To generate features suitable for machine learning of these semantic categories, we used a small set of lexico-syntactic relationships, each defined with respect to the location of the term in a sentence:

prev_V: the closest token tagged as a verb appearing to the left of the term, along with any prepositions or particles in between. (*cached_in, prioritizing, deal_with*)

prev_VNpr: a construction of the form <verb><NP><prep> appearing to the left of the term. Only the head noun in the NP is retained (*inform|user|of, provides|list|of, causes|increase|in*)

prev_Npr: a construction of the form <noun><prep> appearing to the left of the term. (*restriction_on, applicability_of, time_with*)

---

[1] http://www.uspto.gov/web/offices/ac/ido/oeip/taf/us_stat.htm

[2] We blocked a set of 246 general adjectival modifiers (e.g., *other, suitable, preferred, entire, initial,...*) from participating in terms.

prev_Jpr: a construction of form <adjective> <prep> appearing to the left of the term. (*free_from, desirable_in, unfamiliar_with*)

prev_J: a construction of form <adjective> <prep> appearing to the left of the term. (*excessive, considerable, easy*)

These features were designed to capture specific dependency relations between the term and its premodifiers and dominant verbs, nouns, and adjective phrases. We extracted the features using localized rules rather than create a full dependency parse.[3] One additional feature internal to the term itself was also included: last_word. This simply captured the head term of the noun phrase, which often carries generalizable semantic information about the phrase. Each feature instance was represented as a string comprising a prefix (the feature type) and its value (a token or concatenation of tokens).

### 2.2 Classification

For each term appearing in a subcorpus, the collection of co-occurring features across all documents was assembled into a single weighted feature vector in which the weight captured the number of documents for which the feature occurred in conjunction with the given term. We also calculated the document frequency for each term, as well as its "domain specificity score", a metric reflecting the relative frequency of the term in specialized vs. randomized corpora (see section 3).

In order to avoid the need to create manually labeled training data for each patent domain, we employed bootstrapping, a form of semi-supervised learning in which a small number of labeled features or seed terms are used in an iterative fashion to automaticaly identify other likely diagnostic features or category exemplars. Bootstrapping approaches have previously shown considerable promise in the construction of semantic lexicons (Riloff, 1999; Thelen, 2002, Ziering, 2013). By surveying common prev_V features in a domain-independent patent subcorpus, we selected a small set of domain-independent diagnostic lexico-syntactic features ("seed features") that we felt were strong indicators for each of the three semantic categories. The set of seed features for each category is shown below. Semantically equivalent inflectional variants were also included as features.

Attribute: *improve, optimize, increase, decrease, reduce*

Component: *comprise, contain, encompass, incorporate, use, utilize, consist_of, assembled_of, composed_of*

Task: *accomplish, achieve, enhance, facilitate, assisting_in, employed_in, encounter_in, perform, used_for, utilized_for*

We then utilized these manually labeled generic features to bootstrap larger feature sets $F$ for domain-specific subcorpora. For each term $t$ in a domain-specific subcorpus, we extracted all the manually labeled features that the term co-ocurred with. Any term which co-occurred with at least two labeled feature instances and for which all of its labeled features were of the same class was itself labeled with that class for subsequent use as a seed term $s$ for estimating the parameters of a multinomial naïve Bayes classifier (Manning et al, 2008). Each seed term so selected was represented as a bag of its co-occurring features.

The prior probability of each class and conditional probabilities of each feature given the class were estimated as follows, using Laplace "add one" smoothing to eliminate 0 probabilities:

$$\hat{P}(c_j) = \frac{|S_j|}{|S|}$$

$$\hat{P}(f|c) = \frac{count(f,c) + 1}{count(c) + |F|}$$

[3] The compute time required to produce dependency parses for the quantity of data to be analyzed led to the choice of a "leaner" feature extraction method.

where $S_j$ is the set of seed terms with class label *j*, *S* is the set of all seed terms, *count(f,c)* is the count of co-occurrences of feature *f* with seed terms in class *c*, *count(c)* is the total number of feature co-occurrences with seed terms in class c, and *F* is the set of all features (used for Laplace smoothing).

Using the naïve Bayes conditional independence assumption, the class of each term in a subcorpus was then computed by maximizing the product of the prior probability for a class and the product of the conditional probabilities of the term's features:

$$C = \underset{c \in C}{\operatorname{argmax}} P(c) \prod_{f \in F} P(f|c)$$

Terms for which no diagnostic features existed were labeled as "unknown".

Once the terms in a subcorpus were categorized as *attribute*, *component*, or *task*, the terms identified as attributes were selected as input to a second round of classification.[4] We used the same bootstrapping process as described for the first round, choosing a small set of features highly diagnostic of the polarity of attributes. For positive polarity, the seed features were: *increase, raise, maximize*. For negative polarity: *avoid, lower, decrease, deal_with, eliminate, minimize, reduce, resulting_from, caused_by*. Based on co-occurrence with these features, a set of terms was produced from which parameters for a larger set of features could be estimated, as described above. We then used naïve Bayes classification to label the full set of attribute terms.

## 3 Results

We present results from two domains, health and computer science, using a corpus consisting of all US patent applications submitted in the year 2002. The health subcorpus consisted of 19,800 documents, while the computer science subcorpus contained 51,058 documents. A "generic" corpus composed of 38,482 patents randomly selected from all domains was also constructed for the year for use in computing a "domain specificity score". This score was designed to measure the degree to which a term could be considered part of a specific domain's vocabulary and was computed as the log(probability of term in domain corpus / probability of term in generic corpus). For example, in computer science, the term *encryption technology* earned a domain specificity score of 4.132, while *speed* earned .783 and *color* garnered .022. Using a combination of term frequency (# of documents a term occurs in within a domain) thresholds and domain specificity, one can extract subsets of terms with varying degrees of relevance within a collection.[5]

### 3.1 Attribute/Component/Task (ACT) Classification

The bootstrapping process generated 1,644 features for use in the health domain and 3,200 in computer science. Kullback-Leibler divergence is a commonly used metric for comparing the difference between two probability distributions (Kullback and Leibler, 1951). By computing Kullback-Leibler divergence $D_{KL}(P||Q)$ between the distribution P of classes predicted by each feature (i.e., the probability of the class given the feature alone based on the term seed set labels) and the prior class distribution Q, we could estimate the impact of individual features in the model. Table 1 shows some of the domain-specific features in the health and computer science domains, along with the category each tended to select for.[6]

Using the features generated by bootstrapping, the classifier was able to label 61% of the 1,335,240 terms in health and 81% of the 1,391,402 terms in computer science. The majority of unlabeled terms were extremely low frequency (typically 1). Higher frequency unlabeled terms were typically from categories other than those under consideration here (e.g., *john wiley, j. biochem, 2nd edition*). The distribution of category labels for the health and computer domains is shown in Table 2.

---

[4] We found relatively little evidence of explicit sentiment targeted at component and task aspects in patents and therefore focused our polarity analysis on attributes.

[5] Similar to Velardi's use of "domain relevance" and "consensus" (Velardi, 2001).

[6] Although it is possible to use KL-Divergence for feature selection, it is applied here solely for diagnostic purposes to verify that feature distributions match our intuitions with respect to the classification scheme.

**Table 1. Features highly associated with classes (a[ttribute], c[omponent], t[ask]) in the health and computer science domains, along with an example of a term co-occurring with each feature in some patent.**

| Health | | | Computer Science | | |
|---|---|---|---|---|---|
| **Feature** | **Class** | **Term** | **Feature** | **Class** | **Term** |
| prev_V=performed_during | t | biopsy | prev_V=automates | t | retrieval |
| prev_V=undergone | t | angioplasty | last_word=translation | t | axis translation |
| prev_V=suffer | a | hypertension | prev_Npr=reduction_in | a | power usage |
| prev_Npr=monitoring_of | a | alertness | Prev_Npr=degradation_in | a | audio quality |
| prev_V=binds_to | c | cytokines | prev_V=displayed_on | c | oscillograph |
| prev_Npr=salts_of | c | saccharin | last_word=information | c | customer information |

**Table 2. Number and percentage of category labels for health and computer domains (2002)**

| Category | Health | Computer Science |
|---|---|---|
| attribute | 88,860 (10.8 %) | 56,389 (6.5%) |
| component | 680,034 (83.2%) | 716,688 (83.2%) |
| task | 48,002 (5.8 %) | 88,786 (10.3%) |

Tables 3a and 3b show examples of machine-labeled terms for the health and computer science domains. When terms were ranked by frequency, given a relatively relaxed domain specificity threshold (e.g., .05 for health), the top terms tended to capture broad semantic types relevant to the domain. As this threshold was increased (e.g., to 1.0 for health), the terms increased in specialization within each class.[7] As the table entries show, while the classification is not perfect, most terms fit the definitions of their respective classes. Note that in the health domain in particular, many of the "components" reflect objects acted upon by the invention, not just constituents of inventions themselves. Symptoms and diseases are interpreted as attributes because they are often measured according to severity and are targets for reduction.

**Table 3a. Examples of ACT category results for health domain at two levels of domain specificity (ds).**

| Component (ds .05) | (ds 1.0) | Attribute (ds .05) | (ds 1.0) | Task (ds .05) | (ds 1.0) |
|---|---|---|---|---|---|
| patients, tissue, blood, diseases, drugs, skin, catheter, brain, tablets, organs | mitral valve, arterial blood, small incisions, pulmonary veins, anterior chamber, intraocular lens, ultrasound system, ultrasound energy, adenosine triphosphate, bone fragments | disease, infection, symptoms, pain, efficacy, side effects, inflammation, severity, death, blood flow | cosmetic properties, cardiac activity, urination, tissue temperature, gastric emptying, arousal neurotransmitter release, atrial arrhythmias, thrombogenicity ventricular pacing | treatment, administration, therapy, surgery, diagnosis, oral administration, implantation, stimulation, parenteral administration, surgical procedures | invasive procedure, ultrasound imaging, systole, anastomosis, spinal fusion, tissue ablation, image, reconstruction, cardiac pacing, mass analysis, spinal surgery |

[7] The domain specificity thresholds chosen here differ between domains in order to compensate for the influence of the size of each domain's subcorpus on the terminology mix in the "generic" domain corpus against which domain specificity is measured. In the future, we plan to compensate directly for these size disparities in the score computation.

**Table 3b. Examples of ACT category results for computer domain at two levels of domain specificity.**

| Component (ds 1.5) | (ds 3.0) | Attribute (ds 1.5) | (ds 3.0) | Task (ds 1.5) | (ds 3.0) |
|---|---|---|---|---|---|
| data, information, network, computer, users, memory, internet, software, program, processor | web applications, object access protocol, loans, memory subsystem, function call, obligations, source file, file formats, lender centralized database | errors, security, real time, traffic, overhead, delays, latency, burden, sales, copyright, protection | interest rate, resource utilization, resource consumption, temporal locality, system errors, transport layer security, performance bottleneck, processor capacity, cpu utilization, shannon limit | access, communication, execution, implementation, communications, management, task, tasks, stores, collection | network environments, business activities, database access, server process, search operation, client 's request, backup operation, project management, program development, document management |

## 3.2 Polarity Classification

For the polarity classification task, the system assigned positive or negative polarity to 80,870 health and 73,289 computer science attributes. While not all the system labeled attributes merited their designation as attributes, the large quantity so labeled in each domain illustrates the vast number of conditions and dimensions for which inventions are striving to "move the needle" one way or the other, relative to attributes in the domain. Examples of the system's polarity decisions are shown in Table 4. The system's labels suggest that the default polarity of attributes in both domains is nearly evenly split.

**Table 4. Examples of (pos)itive and (neg)ative polarity terms in health and computer science domains**

| Domain | # attributes | % of total | Examples |
|---|---|---|---|
| **health** *pos* | 43807 | 54% | ambulation, hemodynamic performance, atrial rate, anticoagulant activity, coaptation, blood oxygen saturation |
| *neg* | 37063 | 46% | bronchospasm, thrombogenicity, ventricular pacing, withdrawal symptoms, fibrin formation, cardiac dysfunction |
| **computer science** *pos* | 32291 | 44% | transport layer security, processor capacity, cpu utilization, routability, network speeds, microprocessor performance |
| *neg* | 40998 | 56% | identity theft, deadlocks, system overhead, memory fragmentation, risk exposure, bus contention, software development costs, network latencies, data entry errors |

## 4 Evaluation and discussion

In order to evaluate the classification output, we first selected a subset of terms within each domain as candidates for evaluation based on the twin criteria of document frequency and domain specificity. That is, we wished to concentrate on terms with sufficient presence in the corpus as well as terms that were likely to express concepts of particular relevance to the domain. Using a frequency threshold of 10 this yielded 19,088 terms for the health corpus and 35,220 for computer science with domain specificity scores above .05 and 1.5 respectively. For each domain, two judges annotated approximately 150 random term instances with ACT judgments and approximately 100 machine-labeled attributes for polarity. The annotation tool displayed each term along with five random sentences from the corpus that contained the term, and asked the judge to choose the best label, given the contexts provided. An "other" option was available if the term fit none of the target categories. For the polarity task, the "other" label included cases where the attribute was neutral, could not be assigned a polarity, or was improperly assigned the category "attribute". An adjudicated gold standard was compared to system labels to measure precision and recall, as shown in table 5.

**Table 5a. Health domain: precision, recall and F-score for ACT and polarity classification tasks**

| Task | Category | Precision | Recall | F-score |
|---|---|---|---|---|
| **ACT** | attribute | .70 | .44 | .54 |
| | component | .76 | 1.0 | .86 |
| | task | .86 | .29 | .43 |
| **Polarity** | positive | .53 | .85 | .65 |
| | negative | .77 | .93 | .84 |

**Table 5b. Computer domain: precision, recall and F-score for ACT and polarity classification tasks**

| Task | Category | Precision | Recall | F-score |
|---|---|---|---|---|
| **ACT** | attribute | .80 | .62 | .70 |
| | component | .86 | .96 | .90 |
| | task | .43 | .33 | .38 |
| **Polarity** | positive | .67 | .88 | .76 |
| | negative | .75 | .86 | .80 |

Although the size of the evaluation set is small, we can make some observations from this sample. Precision in most cases is strong, which is important for the intended use of this data to characterize trends along each dimension using terminology statistics over time. The lower scores for tasks within the ACT classification may reflect the fact that the distinction between component and task is not always clear cut. The term "antivirus protection", for example, describes a task but it is classified by the system as a component because it occurs with features like "prev_V=distribute" and "prev_V=provided_with", which outweigh the contribution of the feature "last_word=protection" to select for the type task. To capture such cases of role ambiguity, it may be reasonable to assign some terms to multiple classes when the conditional probabilities for the two most probable classes are very close (as they are in this case). It may also be possible to integrate other forms of evidence, such as syntactic coordination patterns (Zierning, 2013) to refine system decisions.

One shortcoming of the current polarity classifier is that it does not attempt to identify attributes for which the polarity is neutral or dependent upon further context within the domain. For example, the attribute "body weight gain" is labeled as a negative. However, in the context of premature birth or cancer recovery, it may be actually be a positive attribute. Testing whether an attribute co-occurs with conflicting features (e.g., prev_V=increase and prev_V=decrease) could help spot such cases.

## 5 Related work

Text mining from patents has focused on identifying domain keywords and terminology for analytics (Tseng, 2007). Velardi's (2001) approach, using statistics to determine domain relevance and consensus is very similar to that adopted here. We have also drawn inspiration from sentiment analysis, proposing an ontology for patents that reflects their review-like qualities (Liu, 2012). Most relevant is the work on discovering aspects and opinions relating to a particular subject such as a camera or restaurant (Kobayashi, 2007). There are many subtleties that have been studied in opinion mining research that we have finessed in our research here, such as detecting implicit sentiment and attributes not expressed as noun phrases. Wilson et al (2005, 2009) addressed the larger problem of determining contextual polarity for subjective expressions in general, putting considerable effort into the compilation of subjectivity clues and annotations. In contrast, our aim was to test whether we could substantially reduce the annotation effort when the task is focused on polarity labeling of attributes within patents. We hypothesized that the specialized role of patents might permit a more lightweight approach amenable to bootstrapping from a very small set of annotations and feature types.

Bootstrapping has been successfully applied to developing semantic lexicons containing a variety of concept types (Riloff, 1999; Thelen, 2002). It is often applied iteratively to learn new discriminative features after a set of high probability categorized terms are identified during an earlier round. While this increases recall, it also runs the risk of semantic drift if some terms are erroneously labeled. Given that the majority of unlabeled terms after a single round in our system are either extremely low frequency or not relevant to our ontology, we have not felt a need to run multiple iterations. Zierning (2013) used bootstrapping to identify instances of the classes *substance* and *disease* in patents, exploiting the tendency of syntactic coordination to relate noun phrases of the same semantic type. Given the general nature of coordination, a similar approach could be used to find corroborating evidence for the classifications that our system produces.

## 6 Conclusion

We have described an approach to text data mining from patents that strikes a middle ground between undifferentiated keywords and rich, domain specific ontologies. Motivated by the interpretation of patents as "positive reviews", we have made use of generic lexico-syntactic features common across patent domains to bootstrap domain-specific classifiers capable of organizing terms according to their roles as components, tasks and attributes with polarity. Although the majority of keywords in a domain are categorized as components, the ontology puts tasks and attributes on an equal footing with components, thereby shifting the emphasis from devices and processes to the goals, obstacles and targets of inventions, information which could be valuable for analysts attempting to detect trends and make forecasts. In addition to more rigorous evaluation and tuning, future research directions include testing the approach across a wider range of technology domains, incorporation into time series analysis for forecasting, and mining relationships between terms from different categories to provide an even richer terminological landscape for analysts to work with.

## Acknowledgements

This research is supported by the Intelligence Advanced Research Projects Activity (IARPA) via Department of Interior National Business Center (DoI/NBC) contract number D11PC20154. The U.S. Government is authorized to reproduce and distribute reprints for Governmental purposes notwithstanding any copyright annotation thereon. Disclaimer: The views and conclusions contained herein are those of the authors and should not be interpreted as necessarily representing the official policies or endorsements, either expressed or implied, of IARPA, DoI/NBC, or the U.S. Government.

## References

de Miranda, G. M. Coelho, Dos, and L. F. Filho. (2006) Text mining as a valuable tool in foresight exercises: A study on nanotechnology. Technological Forecasting and Social Change, 73(8):1013–1027.

Kobayashi, N., Inui, K. and Matsumoto, Y. (2007) Extracting aspect-evaluation and aspect-of relations in opinion mining, Proceedings of the 2007 Joint Conference on Empirical Methods in Natural Language Processing and Computational Natural Language Learning, Prague, Czech Republic, pp. 1065–1074.

Kullback, S. and Leibler, R. (1951). "On Information and Sufficiency". Annals of Mathematical Statistics 22 (1): 79–86.

Liu, B. (2012): Sentiment Analysis and Opinion Mining. Synthesis Lectures on Human Language Technologies, Morgan & Claypool Publishers.

Manning, C., Raghavan, P. and Schütze, H. (2008) Introduction to Information Retrieval. Cambridge University Press.

Riloff, E. and Jones, R. (1999) Learning dictionaries for information extraction by multi-level bootstrapping. In Proceedings of the 16th National Conference on Artificial Intelligence and the 11th Innovative Applications of Artificial Intelligence Conference, pp. 474–479.

Riloff, E. and Shepherd, J. (1997) A corpus-based approach for building semantic lexicons. In Proceedings of the Second Conference on Empirical Methods in Natural Language Processing, pp. 117–124.

Shih, M.J., Liu, D.R., and Hsu, M.L. (2008) Mining Changes in Patent Trends for Competitive Intelligence. PAKDD 2008: 999-1005.

Sheremetyeva S. 2009. An Efficient Patent Keyword Extractor As Translation Resource Proceedings of the 3rd Workshop on Patent Translation in conjunction with MT-Summit XII Ottawa, Canada.

Thelen, M. and Riloff, E. (2002) A bootstrapping method for learning semantic lexicons using extraction pattern contexts. In Proceedings of the Conference on Empirical Methods in Natural Language.

Toutanova, K., Klein, D., Manning, C. and Singer, Y. (2003) Feature-Rich Part-of-Speech Tagging with a Cyclic Dependency Network. In Proceedings of HLT-NAACL 2003, pp. 252-259.

Tseng, Y.-H., Lin, C.-J., and Lin, Y.-I. (2007). Text mining techniques for patent analysis. Information Processing & Management, 43(5):1216 – 1247.

Velardi, P., Fabriani, P. and Missikoff, M. (2001) FOIS '01 Proceedings of the international conference on Formal Ontology in Information Systems - Volume 2001, pp. 270-284.

Wilson, T., Wiebe, J and Hoffmann, P. (2005). Recognizing Contextual Polarity in Phrase-Level Sentiment Analysis. Joint Human Language Technology Conference and the Conference on Empirical Methods in Natural Language Processing (HLT-EMNLP-2005).

Wilson, T., Wiebe, J and Hoffmann, P. (2009). Recognizing Contextual Polarity: an exploration of features for phrase-level sentiment analysis. Computational Linguistics 35(3).

Woon, W. L., Henschel, A., and Madnick, S. (2009) A Framework for Technology Forecasting and Visualization. Working Paper CISL# 2009-11 , Massachusetts Institute of Technology.

Yang, S.Y., Lin, S.Y., Lin, S. N., Lee, C. F., Cheng, S. L., and Soo, V. W. (2008) Automatic extraction of semantic relations from patent claims. International Journal of Electronic Business Management, Vol. 6, No. 1, pp. 45-54 (2008) 45.

Ziering, P., van der Plas, L. and Schütze, H. (2013) Bootstrapping Semantic Lexicons for Technical Domains. In Proceedings of the Sixth International Joint Conference on Natural Language Processing, pp. 844–848, Nagoya, Japan, October 2013. Asian Federation of Natural Language Processing.

# Pre-reordering Model of Chinese Special Sentences for Patent Machine Translation

Renfen Hu, Zhiying Liu, Lijiao Yang, Yaohong Jin
*Institute of Chinese Information Processing,*
*Beijing Normal University,*
*Beijing 100875, China*
bnuhurenfen@126.com
{liuzhy,yanglijiao,jinyaohong}@bnu.edu.cn

## Abstract

Chinese prepositions play an important role in sentence reordering, especially in patent texts. In this paper, a rule-based model is proposed to deal with the long distance reordering of sentences with special prepositions. We firstly identify the prepositions and their syntax levels. After that, sentences are parsed and transformed to be much closer to English word order with reordering rules. After integrating our method into a patent MT system, the reordering and translation results of source language are effectively improved.

## 1 Introduction

As typical technical documents, Patents have proven to be suitable for automatic translation for its strict format and united writing pattern (Jin and Liu, 2011), and patent machine translation (MT) is one of the major application fields of MT. However, sentences in patent are known for their complicated structures with multiple verbs and prepositions. Some Chinese prepositions are used to change the original S-V-O order of sentences, such as 把(BA), which make it more difficult for reordering in Chinese-English machine translation. In ancient Chinese, these prepositions are mostly verbs or other notional words, and in modern Chinese they became grammatical markers after diachronic grammaticalization. Huang(1998) and Miao(2005) discussed the reordering function of these prepositions, and defined them as Logic-0 (L0) words.

A linguistic study by Zhang(2001) shows that more than 20% Chinese sentences are reordered by the prepositions, including 把(BA), 将(JIANG), 向(XIANG), 与(YU), 对(DUI), 给(GEI), 被(BEI), 由(YOU) and 为(WEI). After analyzing sentences of 500 Chinese patent documents, we find that L0 words appear more frequently in patent texts. Sentences with 1 L0 word occupy 30.75%, sentences with 2 L0 word occupy 9.05%, and sentences with ⩾3 L0 words occupy 2.10%. Therefore, Chinese special sentences with L0 words are concerned in this paper, and we will present a pre-reordering model of these special sentences for patent translation.

Figure 1 and Figure 2 show an example illustrating some of the differences in word order between Chinese and English.

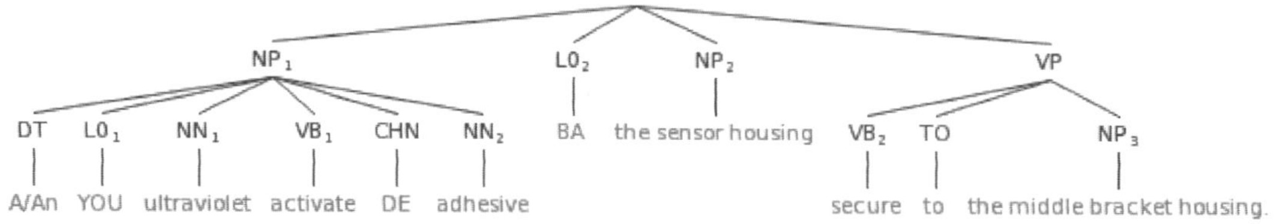


Figure 1. Chinese syntax tree of the example sentence





*Proceedings of SADAATL 2014*, pages 40–47,
Dublin, Ireland, August 24, 2014.

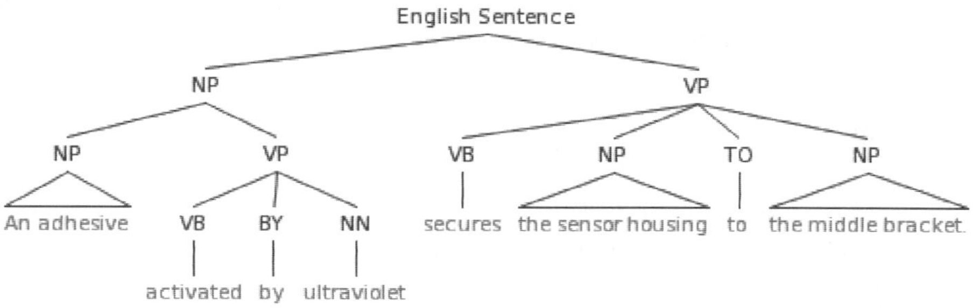

Figure 2. English syntax tree of the example sentence

The example shows a Chinese sentence whose literal translation in English is:

A/an **YOU(L0)** ultraviolet activate DE adhesive **BA(L0)** the sensor housing secure to the middle bracket housing. *(一种由紫外线激活的粘合剂把传感器壳体固定在中支架上。)*

And where a natural translation in English would be

*An adhesive activated by ultraviolet secures the sensor housing to the middle bracket.*

As exemplified by this sentence, differences of word order between Chinese and English are determined by BA and YOU, and they are in two different levels in the syntax tree.

In order to produce a good English translation, we firstly identify L0 words in two levels, and parse the sentence into chunks with core predicate and L0 words. Based on the sentence parsing, chunks are reordered according to related rules, transforming Chinese special sentence into a word order that is closer to that of English. After integrating into a patent MT system running in SIPO (State Intellectual Property Office of People's Republic of China)[1], our model performs better than the baseline system and Google Translate in an open test, and it greatly improves the performance of patent translation.

After a discussion of related work in section 2 and an introduction to semantic features in section 3, we will discuss the reordering model in section 4. Section 5 presents the processing steps, and section 6 gives the experiment and evaluation. Finally we draw some conclusions in section 7.

## 2 Related Works

Nowadays statistical machine translation (SMT) is the most widely used method in MT field, and reordering approaches are proved necessary in SMT performance(Xia and McCord, 2004; Collins et al, 2005). Most SMT systems employ some mechanism that allows reordering of the source language during translation(Wang et al, 2007), and researchers find that reordering based on syntactic analysis are effective for handling systematic differences in word order between source and target languages (Xia and McCord, 2004; Collins et al, 2005).

Although sentence structure of source language has been taken into consideration, most SMT systems make use of syntax information in decoding stage (Lin, 2004; Ding and Palmer, 2005; Quirk et al, 2005; Liu et al, 2006, Huang et al, 2006). Wang et al.(2007) firstly incorporate a Chinese syntactic reordering method into preprocessing stage of a statistical MT system, and achieve a significant improvement in reordering accuracy. Zhang et al.(2007) propose a chunk-level method with reordering rules automatically learned from source-side chunks, it shows improvement of BLEU score and better computational efficiency than reordering during decoding in Chinese-English task. Genzel(2010) applies this approach to 8 different language pairs in phrase-based machine translation, and demonstrates that many important order transformations (SVO to SOV or VSO, head modifier, verb movement) can be captured by this approach. An automatic reordering model in preprocessing also works effectively in Japanese-English patent machine translation(Katz-Brown and Collins, 2008).

However, existing methods face difficulties in Chinese-English patent translation. A Chinese patent sentence often contains multiple nested phrases with a number of verbs, prepositions and correlations. In addition to that, ambiguity of L0 words turns it more difficult for language parsers to make syntax analysis. Moreover, reordering rules can hardly be automatically learned from patent sentences with complicate structures. To deal with the long-distance reordering of special sentences in patent texts,

[1] http://c2e.cnpat.com.cn/sesame.aspx

we must fully consider semantic features of L0 words, including their positions, correlations, functions, ambiguities and levels. With the identification of L0 words and their levels, we can parse and reorder a sentence more explicitly.

## 3 Semantic Features

A linguistic survey shows that S-V-O account for more than 75% of the world's languages, suggesting it may be somehow more initially "obvious" to human psychology(Crystal, 1997). Both modern Chinese and English are S-V-O languages, however, word order in Chinese sentence is often changed by L0 words to emphasize a part of the sentence, or to make nuance of the meaning. Our work aims at reordering Chinese special sentences to organize phrases or words in English order without L0 words. We have defined 9 Chinese prepositions as L0 words in Section 1. To deal with the reordering of Chinese special sentences with these words, we use semantic features from the Hierarchical Network of Concepts theory (HNC theory). In the opinion of HNC researchers, L0 words and verbs are important clues of syntactic and semantic analysis(Jin, 2010). Therefore, we will introduce the features of L0 words and verbs in the following part.

### 3.1 Types of L0 Words

According to HNC theory, L0 words can be divided into 2 types, L01 and L02(Huang, 1998; Miao, 2005).

*Sentence 1 Tom eats a banana.*

*Sentence 2 Tom **BA(把)** a banana eat.*

*Sentence 3 A banana **BEI(被)** Tom eat.*

In sentence 1, we know that *Tom* is an agent, and *a banana* is a patient. Sentence 2 and 3 are expressing the same meaning in Chinese with L0 words. It can be seen that the two L0 words reorder the sentence in different ways, BA(把) just exchanges the location of the predicate and the object, while BEI(被) changes the sentence from active to passive voice. BA(把) is a L02 word, and BEI(被) belongs to L01. The types of L0 words are presented in Table 1.

| Types | Members | Semantic format | Example sentence |
|---|---|---|---|
| L01 | 被 (BEI), 由(YOU) , 为(WEI) | Patient+L01+Agent+Predicate | Tom BA(把) a banana eat. |
| L02 | 把(BA), 将(JIANG),向(XIANG), 对(DUI), 给(GEI), 与(YU) | Agent+L02+Patient/Recipient+ Predicate | A banana BEI(被) Tom eat. |

Table 1. Two types of L0 words

### 3.2 Levels of L0 Words

By comparing the syntax trees in Figure 1 and Figure 2, we can note that *YOU(由)* appears in a NP(noun phrase), while *BA(把)* appears independently in the sentence. To distinguish the two kinds of L0 words, we define a LEVEL value for L0 words according to their node locations in the syntax tree. L0 word as LEVEL[1] is a child node of S(sentence), while L0 as LEVEL[2] is a child node of NP.

Accordingly, our reordering model includes two modules, the reordering of Sentence with L0 as LEVEL[1] and the reordering of NP with L0 as LEVEL[2]. Therefore, we need firstly identify the level of each L0 word in sentences.

### 3.3 Collocation with Predicates

More than one L0 word may appear in a sentence, but each L0 is in combination with a certain predicate. As exemplified by the sentence in Figure 1, *YOU(由)* goes with the verb *activate*, while *BA(把)* goes with the verb *secure*. For this reason, L0 and its level can also help to determine the core predicate when a sentence has more than one verb.

Predicates are also classified into 2 types according to their levels in the syntax tree. We give 2 simple English sentences to explain the 2 types, P1 and P2.

*Sentence 4 Bob tells(P1) me a secret.*

*Sentence 5 A secret told(P2) by Bob is spreading(P1).*

As labelled in the 2 examples, P1 refers to the core predicate, and P2 is the predicate in a noun phrase. L0 word in level 1 is in combination with P1, while L0 word in level 2 is in combination with P2. The identification of the two types of predicates is introduced in detail by Zhu(2012). Table 2 shows the levels of L0 words and their collocations with predicates.

| L0 Level | Parent Node | Collocated Predicates |
|---|---|---|
| LEVEL[1] | Sentence | P1 |
| LEVEL[2] | NP | P2 |

Table 2. The collocations of L0 words and predicates

## 4 Reordering Model of Chinese Special Sentences

Our model aims at the reordering of Chinese special sentences with L0 words for patent machine translation. With the identification of predicates, L0 words, and their levels (Hu et al, 2013), we can parse the sentence and get a Chinese syntax tree. In this section, we will firstly introduce the transformations and rules in the reordering, and then discuss how to transform the syntax tree to make the word order closer to English sentence. Semantic features of L0 and verbs that we discussed in section 3 will be applied into the model.

### 4.1 Transformations in the Reordering

There are 5 types of transformations in the processing of our reordering model.

**Deletion:** L0 words are Chinese prepositions, so we need to delete or substitute them at first.

**Addition:** Some L0 words have no real meanings, such as 把(BA) and 将(JIANG), we can make other transformations after deleting them. However, some L0 words have preposition meanings that cannot be neglected, so we need to add English prepositions to the new tree. This operation can also be interpreted as "substitution".

**Copying:** In long distance reordering, some chunks do not need any transformation, so we just copy it to the new syntax tree.

**Rearrangement:** We need to rearrange the chunks to make the word order closer to English.

**Voice Transition:** A research by Liu(2011) shows that 95.6% English patent sentences use passive voice. Considering the voice difference between Chinese and English, we transform some active sentences to passive sentences.

### 4.2 Rule Description

The above 5 transformations are integrated in our reordering rules. We will describe how rules work with Rule 1 as an example.

*Rule 1:*

*(b){(-1)CHK[NP]}+(0)CHN[ 由 ]&CHK[L0] +(1)CHK[NP]+(2)CHK[P1]&VV[2]=>(-1)+ COPY[-1,0]+ DEL_NODE(0)+(2){VOI=P}+ ADD_NODE(ENG=[by])+(1)*

Each reordering rule includes a left part and a right part, with arrow "=>" as the boundary. *CHK* is short for *chunk*, and *VV* is short for *verb valency*, which is a feature for verbs in our semantic knowledge base. The left part describes chunks in the Chinese syntax tree, and each chunk is marked with a node number. The right part describes the reordering result. In Rule 1, L0 *由* is deleted, English preposition *by* is added, *P1* is transformed to passive voice, contents between node 0 and node 1 are copied to the new syntax tree, and the chunks orders are rearranged from *(-1)+(0)+(1)+(2)* to *(-1)+COPY[-1,0]+(2)+by+(1)*.

### 4.3 Reordering Analysis

After an introduction to our rules and their functions, we will present two examples to illustrate the reordering work.

#### 4.3.1 Reordering of Sentences

After analyzing sentences from 500 patent texts, 51 rules are made to deal with the sentences with L0 as LEVEL[1]. We will discuss this reordering work with Sentence 6 as an example.

*Sentence 6 BA data to be transmitted divide into plural blocks. (**把**待发送的数据分为多个数据块。)*

After identification of L0 words and predicates, we can get a syntax tree as shown in Figure 3.

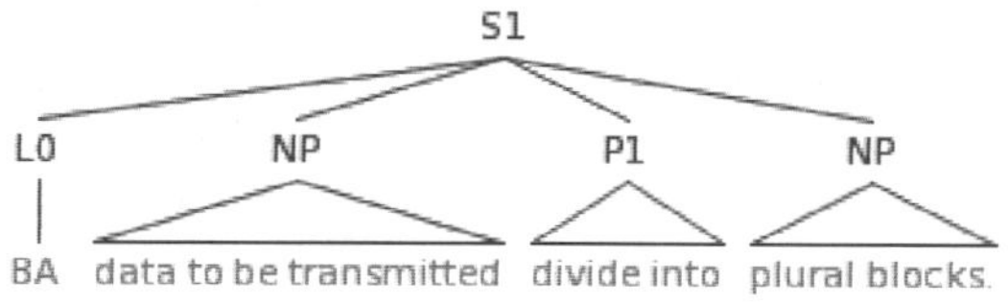


Figure 3. Syntax tree of Sentence 6 before reordering

In reordering stage, the sentence will be transformed by matching the following rule.

*Rule 2:*

*(b){!CHK[NP]}+(0)CHN[ 把 ]&CHK[L0]+(1)CHK[NP]+(2)CHK[P1]&VV[3]+(3)CHK[NP] => DEL_NODE(0)+(1)+(2){VOI=P}+(3)*

After the transformation, we get a new syntax tree as shown in Figure 4.

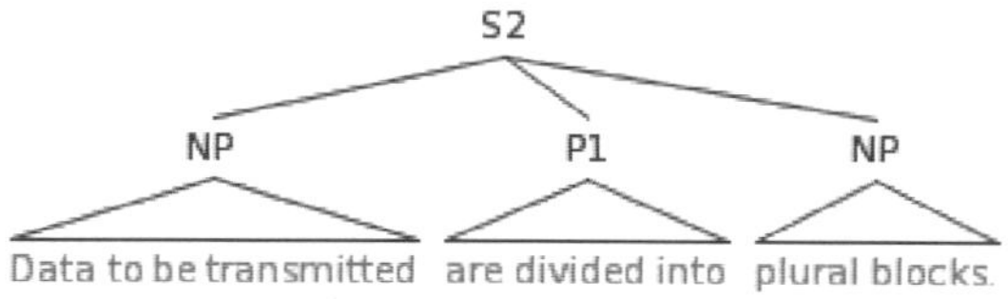


Figure 4. Syntax tree of sentence 6 after reordering

#### 4.3.2 Reordering of Noun Phrases

In patent texts, noun phrases are often long and complicated, as well as sentences. We have made 31 rules to deal with the reordering of NPs with L0 words. Taking Sentence 7 as an example, we will present the reordering of NPs.

*Sentence 7 The fastener has YU mounting hole formed on the blade fit DE projection. (紧固件具有**与**锯条上安装孔相配合的凸台。)*

*YU mounting hole formed on the blade fit DE projection* is a NP with L0. In this NP, *YU* is identified as L0 in LEVEL[2], and *fit* is P2 in combination with L0. By matching Rule 3, we can transform the syntax tree in Figure 5 to a new syntax tree in Figure 6.

*Rule 3:*

*(-3){CHK[L0]&CHN[ 与 ]}+(-2)CHK[NP]+(-1)CHK[P2]+(0)CHN[ 的 ] +(1)CHK[NP] => DEL_NODE(-3)+(1)+ADD_NODE(ENG=[which])+(-1){VOI=P}+ADD_NODE(ENG=[with])+(-2)+ DEL_NODE(0)*

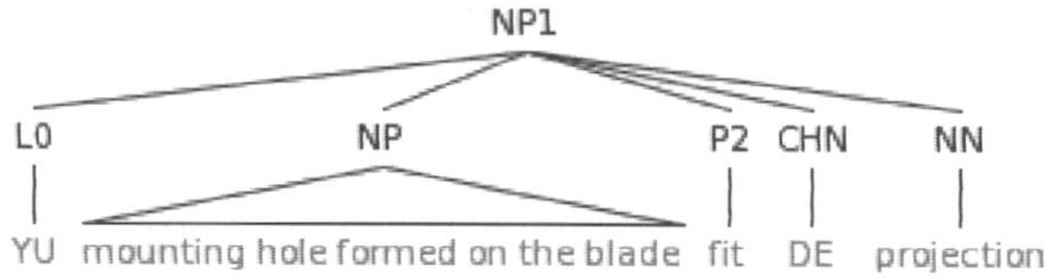


Figure 5. Syntax tree of the NP before reordering

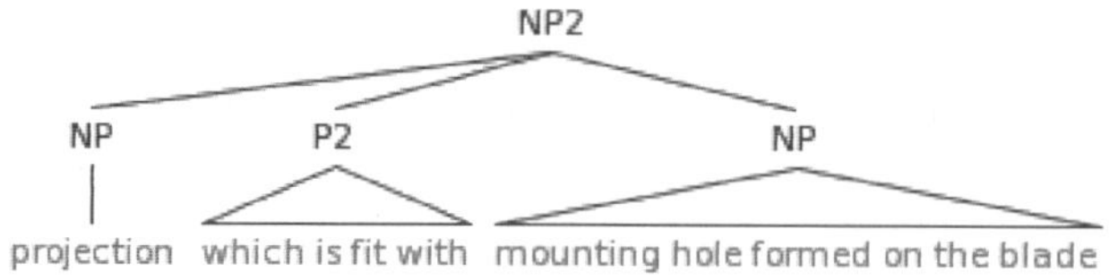


Figure 6. Syntax tree of the NP after reordering

Obviously, the word order in Figure 6 is much closer to English sentence than in Figure 5.

## 5 Processing Steps

The reordering is processed in steps as follows.

**Step 1:** To preprocess the Chinese sentence, including word segmentation and word-sense-disambiguation.

**Step 2:** To identify predicates, L0 words and their levels.

**Step 3:** To segment the sentence into chunks with L0 words(Level[1]) and predicates(P1) as boundaries.

**Step 4:** To reorder the sentences with L0 words(LEVEL[1]) based on transformation rules.

**Step 5:** To reorder the NPs with L0 words(LEVEL[2]) based on transformation rules.

**Step 6:** To generate a new syntax tree closer to English language order.

## 6 Experiment and Discussion

The experiment takes 500 authentic patent texts provided by SIPO (State Intellectual Property Office of China) as the training set. The evaluation will use the development data for the NTCIR-9 Patent Machine Translation Pilot Task[2], containing 2,000 bilingual Chinese-English sentence pairs.

After integrating into a rule-based patent machine translation system(Zhu et al, 2012), we will take a closed test on the training set, and an open test on the evaluation set. To evaluate the effects of the reordering rules, precision and recall are calculated by manual evaluation for both two tests. In the open test, NIST (Doddington et al, 2002) and BLEU score (Papineni et al, 2002) are also employed to evaluate the translation performance. Table 3 shows the result of the closed test.

| Types | Precision (%) | Recall (%) | F-score (%) |
|---|---|---|---|
| Sentences with L0 | 97.14 | 88.20 | 92.45 |
| NPs with L0 | 91.80 | 73.91 | 81.89 |

Table 3. Experiment Result on the Training Set

It can be seen from table 3 that the reordering rules have higher accuracy and reliability than coverage, and the module of sentence reordering performs better than NP reordering.

In the open test, comparison is made as shown in table 4. RB-MT is the baseline system. RB-MT+PRM is the system integrated with our reordering model. GOOGLE is an online statistical MT system, the reordering result of which is inferred from its translation result. Table 4 shows the comparison in reordering of the three systems.

| Systems | Precision (%) | Recall (%) | F-score (%) |
|---|---|---|---|
| RB-MT | 71.23 | 62.02 | 66.31 |
| RB-MT+PRM | 88.11 | 75.90 | 81.55 |
| GOOGLE | 60.71 | 51.20 | 55.56 |

Table 4. Compared Result of the Open Test

The result of the open test shows that our model has effectively improved the reordering result of Chinese special sentences, and Google performs poorly in this test. It is mainly because statistical methods face difficulties in long distance reordering, and technical texts (including patent texts) account for a fairly low proportion in the training bilingual corpus. Thus, our method is advantageous in processing technical texts with long and complicated sentences.

After calculating the precision and recall, we give NIST and BLEU scores of the three systems. In order to learn the impact of the pre-reordering model in statistical machine translation, we also put the

[2] http://research.nii.ac.jp/ntcir/ntcir-9/

pre-reordered Chinese sentences into GOOGLE Translate and get the English translation result as a comparison. The reordered sentences are obtained from intermediate outputs of RB-MT+PRM system.

| Systems | NIST | BLEU(%) |
|---|---|---|
| RB-MT | 4.85 | 19.97 |
| RB-MT+PRM | 5.36 | 22.33 |
| GOOGLE | 7.84 | 35.24 |
| GOOGLE+PRM | 7.90 | 36.07 |

Table 5. NIST and BLEU-4 Scores

From table 5, we can see that after integrating the reordering model, NIST score of RB-MT system has increased by 10.52%, and BLEU score has increased by 11.82%. Google also has an improvement when input texts are replaced by reordered sentences. Since statistical machine translation has already worked efficiently in short-distance reordering, its improvement is slighter than rule-based systems.

Besides, Google Translate performs better in this evaluation. It is mainly because the corpus domain is not limited, unknown terms or entities may result in a bad translation performance for rule-based systems. In addition, the module of word selection in RB-MT needs to be improved urgently. From the experiment, we also find that the pre-reordering model is strongly dependent on the completeness of rules and the accuracy of the knowledge base, which still need to be improved in the future work.

## 7 Conclusion

To deal with the reordering of Chinese special sentences, we use a source-language parser to distinguish the levels of L0 words and make transformations in the syntax tree.

Our model improves the performance of patent machine translation. In the future, the rule set and knowledge base need to be improved, and our reordering method can be extended to machine translation of technical texts in other fields.


## ACKNOWLEDGMENT

The authors are grateful to National High Technology Research and Development Program of China (No. 2012AA011104) for financial support.


## Reference


Collins M., Koehn P., and Ivona K. 2005. *Clause restructuring for statistical machine translation*. In Proceedings of ACL: 531–540.

Crystal D. 1997. *The Cambridge Encyclopedia of Language*, 2nd ed. Cambridge University Press, Cambridge, UK.

Ding Y. and Palmer M. 2005. *Machine translation using probabilistic synchronous dependency insertion grammars*. In Proceedings of ACL: 541–548.

Doddington G. 2002. *Automatic evaluation of machine translation quality using n-gram co-occurrence statistics*, In Proceedings of Human Language Technology Research: 138-145.

Genzel D. 2010. *Automatically learning source-side reordering rules for large scale machine translation*. In Proceedings of COLING: 376-384.

Hu R.F., Zhu Y., and Jin Y.H. 2013. *Semantic Analysis of Chinese Prepositional Phrases for Patent Machine Translation*. Chinese Computational Linguistics and Natural Language Processing Based on Naturally Annotated Big Data. Springer Berlin Heidelberg.

Huang Z.Y. 1998. *HNC (Hierarchical network of concepts) Theory (in Chinese)*. Tsinghua University Press, Beijing, China.

Huang L. Knight K. and Joshi A. 2006. *Statistical syntax-directed translation with extended domain of locality*. In Proceedings of AMTA:223-226.

Jin Y.H. 2010. *A hybrid-strategy method combining semantic analysis with rule-based MT for patent machine translation*. In Proceedings of NLP-KE: 1-4.

Jin Y.H. and Liu Z. Y. 2011. *Improving Chinese-English patent machine translation using sentence segmentation*, In Proceedings of NLP-KE: 620-625.

Katz-Brown J. and Collins M. 2008. *Syntactic reordering in preprocessing for Japanese→English translation: MIT system description for NTCIR-7 patent translation task*. In Proceedings of NTCIR-7 Workshop Meeting: 409-414.

Lin D. 2004. *A path-based transfer model for machine translation*. In Proceedings of COLING, Geneva, Switzerland: 625–630.

Liu Y., Liu Q. and Lin S. 2006. *Tree-to-string alignment template for statistical machine translation*. In Proceedings of ACL: 609–616.

Liu Z.Y. 2011. *The research of passive voice in Chinese-English patent machine translation*. In Proceedings of NLP-KE: 300-303.

Miao C.J. 2005. *HNC (Hierarchical network of concepts) theory introduction (in Chinese)*. Tsinghua University Press, Beijing, China.

Papineni K., Roukos S., Ward T, et al. 2002. *BLEU: a method for automatic evaluation of machine translation*. In Proceedings of ACL: 311-318.

Quirk C. Menezes A. and Cherry C. *Dependency tree let translation: Syntactically informed phrasal SMT*. In Proceedings of ACL: 271–279.

Wang C. , Collins M. and Koehn P. 2007. *Chinese Syntactic Reordering for Statistical Machine Translation*. In Proceedings of Joint Conference on Empirical Methods in Natural Language Processing and Computational Natural Language Learning: 737–745.

Xia F. and McCord M. 2004. *Improving a statistical MT system with automatically learned rewrite patterns*. In Proceedings of ACL: 508.

Zhang Y., Zens R. and Ney H. 2007. *Chunk-level reordering of source language sentences with automatically learned rules for statistical machine translation*. In Proceedings of the NAACL-HLT: 1-8.

Zhang Y.H. 2001. *Format transformation in English-Chinese translation (in Chinese)*. HNC theory and language research. Wuhan University of Technology Press, Wuhan, China.

Zhu Y. and Jin Y.H. 2012. *A Chinese-English patent machine translation system based on the theory of hierarchical network of concepts*. The Journal of China Universities of Posts and Telecommunications, 19(2): 140-146.

# A Study of Scientific Writing: Comparing Theoretical Guidelines with Practical Implementation

**Mark Kröll***
Know-Center GmbH
Graz, Austria
mkroell@know-center.at

**Gunnar Schulze***
Know-Center GmbH
Graz, Austria
gschulze@know-center.at

**Roman Kern**
Know-Center GmbH
Graz, Austria
rkern@know-center.at

## Abstract

Good scientific writing is a skill researchers seek to acquire. Textbook literature provides guidelines to improve scientific writing, for instance, "use active voice when describing your own work". In this paper we investigate to what extent researchers adhere to textbook principles in their articles. In our analyses we examine a set of selected principles which (i) are general and (ii) verifiable by applying text mining and natural language processing techniques. We develop a framework to automatically analyse a large data set containing $\sim$14.000 scientific articles received from Mendeley and PubMed. We are interested in whether adhering to writing principles is related to scientific quality, scientific domain or gender and whether these relations change over time. Our results show (i) a clear relation between journal quality and scientific imprecision, i.e. journals with low impact factors exhibit higher numbers of imprecision indicators such as number of citation bunches and number of relativating words and (ii) that writing style partly depends on domain characteristics and preferences.

## 1 Introduction

Writing good scientific articles is a skill. Researchers seek to acquire this skill for the purpose of successfully disseminating their ideas to the scientific community. Learning to write good articles is a process that for most of us starts at graduate level and keeps us company in the course of our careers. To advance the learning process, there is (i) plenty of literature out there containing do's and dont's, (ii) seniors administering doses of advice and (iii) entire lectures dedicated to this very subject.

In this paper, we investigate whether researchers do adhere to general writing principles taken from textbook literature. We are interested in whether adhering to writing principles is related to the journal quality, the scientific domain or gender and whether there is a change over time. Doing so allows us to better understand which and to what extent theoretical guidelines are practically implemented. Deviations from textbook literature could be indicators of good practice and if they occur frequently enough, they might also be candidates for textbook updates.

Studying current trends in academic writing (cf. (Tas, 2010)) originates in the domains of pragmatics and linguistics. In this research area we recognize two larger directions. The first one seeks to relate an article's content to scientific concepts, for instance, whether an article contains a theory or not (cf. (Pettigrew et al., 2001)) or to scientific discourse elements, for instance, which paragraphs can be related to categories such as Motivation or Experiment (cf. (Liakata et al., 2012)). The other direction focuses more on organisation and structure including the analysis of entire scientific theses (cf. (Paltridge, 2002)) or the analysis of single structural elements such as the title (cf. (Soler, 2007), (Haggan, 2003)).

In contrast to previous work, we conduct our analyses at a larger scale. We thus develop a framework to automatically analyze large amounts of scientific articles. In our experiments we select writing principles which are on the one hand general and often recommended in textbook literature (cf. (Lebrun, 2007), (Alley, 1996)) and on the other hand automatically retrievable and verifiable by applying text

* These two authors contributed equally to this work.





*Proceedings of SADAATL 2014*, pages 48–55,
Dublin, Ireland, August 24, 2014.

mining and natural language processing techniques. To give an example, the principle "use active voice when describing your own work" is a popular one and can be verified by examining the verb types in the article's abstract, introduction and conclusion. In our study we analyze two data sets - one from Mendeley[1], a popular reference management tool, - one from PubMed[2], a free resource containing citations for biomedical literature. We can observe relations between journal quality and textbook recommendations such as *Avoid Imprecision* and *Engage the Reader*. In addition, the results indicate writing style preferences due to domain characteristics. Our findings show that theoretical guidelines partly concur with practical implementation and thus contribute to better understand the extent to which theory guides praxis and vice versa praxis might guide theory.

The remaining paper is organized as follows: Section 2 provides details on the used data sets as well as the software framework to automate the analysis of scientific articles. Section 3 contains experimental results and discussions of analyzed writing principles. Related work is covered in Section 4 and concluding remarks are presented in Section 5.

## 2 Experimental Setup

### 2.1 Data Sets

For our analyses we used scientific articles from two sources - Mendeley and PubMed - which also provided us with meta data, e.g. name of the conference or journal. Most of the publication organs were journals and we decided to select only journals which had a minimum of 10 articles and for which we could find a respective 5-year impact factor[3]. We decided to conduct our analyses over a 10-year time period from 2001 to 2010, since only in this period articles from both sources were available. In total we experimented with 13866 scientific articles. Grouping them according to scientific quality, domain and gender, we constructed three data sets described in the following:

- Quality: According to the impact factor (IF), we divided the scientific articles into three groups; low IF ranging from 0 to 2.5 (2303 articles), middle IF ranging from 2.5 to 4 (5734 articles) and high IF ranging from 4 to 35 (5829 articles). The ranges were chosen to reflect the journal quality while containing an appropriate (not too small) number of scientific articles per category.

- Domain: We divided the scientific articles by their journal type into two groups: biomedical (7053 articles) and a technical (6813 articles) which contained mainly articles from physics and computer science.

- Gender: We used two gazetteer lists to identify female[4] or male[5] first authors. Since only a part of the authors' first names was unabbreviated, we used a subset of articles for these experiments: number of articles with male first author = 1182, number of articles with female first author = 1990.

### 2.2 Framework

To automatically analyze large amounts of scientific articles, we designed a framework and embedded our analysis algorithms in a Hadoop[6] environment. The environment allows parallelization of processes and thus greatly reduces computation time. We stored the results in a PostgreSQL[7] database for quick access and used various Python packages such as matplotlib[8] for creating graphical representations of our results.

Our first pre-processing step encompassed the extraction of textual content from scientific publications. To automatically extract the content, we used a processing pipeline (cf. (Klampfl et al., 2013))

[1] `http://www.mendeley.com/`
[2] `http://www.ncbi.nlm.nih.gov/pubmed`
[3] `http://www.citefactor.org/impact-factor-list-2012.html`
[4] `http://deron.meranda.us/data/census-dist-female-first.txt`
[5] `http://deron.meranda.us/data/census-dist-male-first.txt`
[6] `http://hadoop.apache.org/`
[7] `http://www.postgresql.org/`
[8] `http://matplotlib.org/`

that applies various machine learning techniques in combination with heuristics to detect the logical structure of a PDF document. Further processing steps included (i) tokenization, (ii) sentence splitting, (iii) stemming, (iv) part-of-speech tagging and (v) chunking. We employed part-of-speech and chunking information in our analyses (see Section 3) to distinguish verb phrases with respect to present vs. past tense as well as active vs. passive voice.

## 3 Analysis of Scientific Literature

In this section we analyze a set of selected writing style principles with respect to *Reader Engagement* and *Imprecision*. Each analysis contains (i) a motivating statement mostly taken from (Lebrun, 2007), (ii) a visual representation of results and (iii) an interpretation of results. During our experiments we could observe that most of the time there were no significant differences between articles written by male and female first authors. We repeated the experiments with a majority criterion of authors, i.e. more female first names or more male first names per article, resulting in similar findings. It appears that both genders adhere to the same guidelines which were standardly used at the time.

### 3.1 Engaging the Reader

In this section we examine different means to engage the reader according to textbook literature including (i) the title, (ii) figures & tables and (iii) a lively writing style based on using present tense and active voice.

#### 3.1.1 Title

The title represents the first point of contact with the reader (and the reviewer) and should ideally be made catchy and standing out. We examine three means to do that: (i) usage of verbs to increase energy, (ii) usage of acronyms to provide a reference shortcut for others and (iii) usage of questions to create a hook. Figure 1 contains average numbers of article titles with respect to these means.

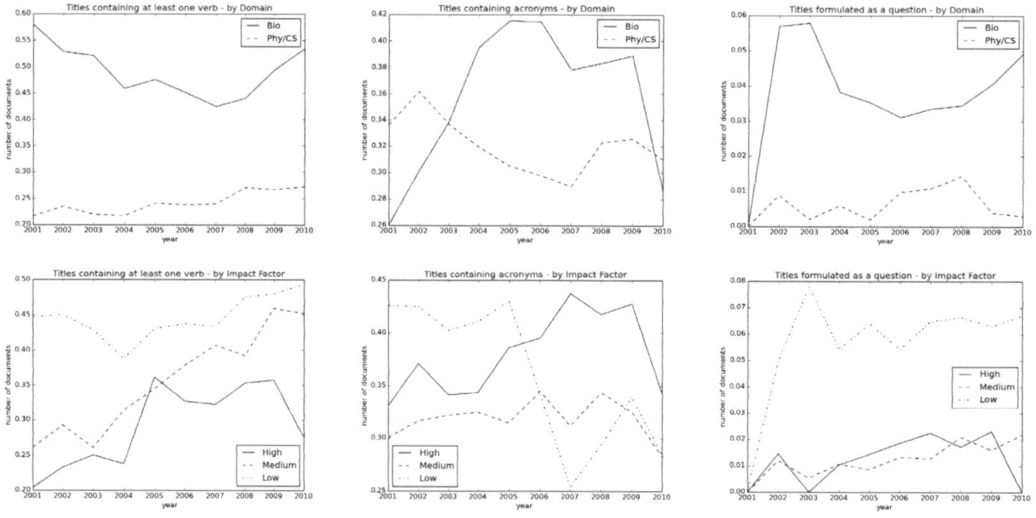


Figure 1: Illustration of (i) titles containting at least one verb (left), (ii) titles containing acronyms (middle) and (iii) titles which contain a question (right) over a ten-year time period. The upper row reflect distinction by domain, the lower row by impact factor. The y-axis represents the average number of article titles exhibiting the respective feature.

The upper left figure in Figure 1 tells us that using verbs in titles is more common among authors in the biomedical domain than in the physics/computer science domain. The lower left figure indicates a trend towards using more verbs in the title over the years independent of the journal quality. The upper, middle figure of Figure 1 shows that using acronyms in titles is more common in the biomedical domain and a possible trend using acronyms at the beginning of the century. The lower figure in the middle indicates an up and down over the years across impact factors. The right figures in Figure 1 tell us that only a low percentage of authors use questions in their titles independent of domain or journal quality.

The numbers corroborate textbook literatures' recommendation of using verbs in the titles as well as using acronyms. A bit surprising is that questions in titles are rarely used, since according to literature they create a mighty hook for the reader. In a next step we intend to relate the title to the content of the abstract and the introduction to answer the question how well the title reflects the article's content.

### 3.1.2 Figures & Tables

Visual representations of results in terms of figures and partly of tables help the reader to reduce reading time. According to (Lebrun, 2007) they even represent visual information burgers which are easy to digest. Figure 2 contains respective average figure and table counts.

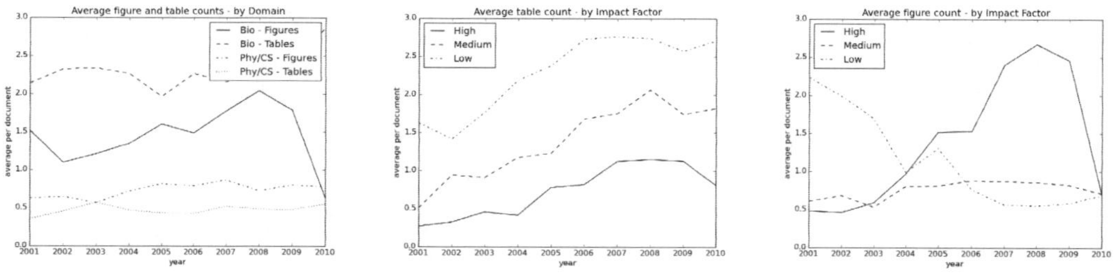


Figure 2: Illustration of average figure and table counts over a ten-year period according to domain (left) and impact factor (middle, right). The y-axis represents the average number of tables/figures per article.

The left figure in Figure 2 illustrates that authors from the biomedical domain use more tables and figures than authors from the physics/computer science domain. The middle and right figure reflect average counts according to impact factor. Journal articles with a high impact factor contain (i) fewer tables than journals with middle or low impact factors and (ii) in general more figures.

From the results in Figure 2 we learn that usage of figures and tables appears to a certain degree be dependent on the domain. In biomedicine, the usage of figures to convey information seems more widespread than in technical domains. We assume even higher figure counts in domains such as chemistry where illustrations, for instance, of molecules are far more frequent. In addition, it seems that authors of high impact journals prefer using figures to using tables probably because the information content is more easily to grasp. Tables appear to be more suited to structure information. In a next step we also intend to analyze figures' and tables' captions with respect to comprehensiveness, i.e. to what extent are captions self-contained?

### 3.1.3 Lively Writing Style

Textbook literature advices authors to formulate their contributions in an active way using active voice and the present tense. To learn more about present tense usage, we simply counted the occurrences of the respective part-of-speech tags[9], i.e. VB, VBP and VBZ. To count occurrences of active voice, we inspected all identified verb chunks whether they contained auxiliary verbs as well as a past participle part-of-speech tag. If they did, we considered them passive voice otherwise active voice. Figure 3 contains average fractions of verb phrases with respect to present tense and active voice.

The upper left figure in Figure 3 illustrates that authors of the physics/computer science domain use a lot more present tense compared to authors from the biomedical domain. The upper right figure indicates that the higher the journal's impact factor the more present tense is used by the authors. The lower left figure indicates that active and passive voice are almost evently distributed throughout article contents with a bit passive predominance. The lower right figure shows no significant difference of using active voice with respect to journal quality. There is but a trend towards using more active voice over the years.

[9] `http://www.cis.upenn.edu/~treebank/home.html`

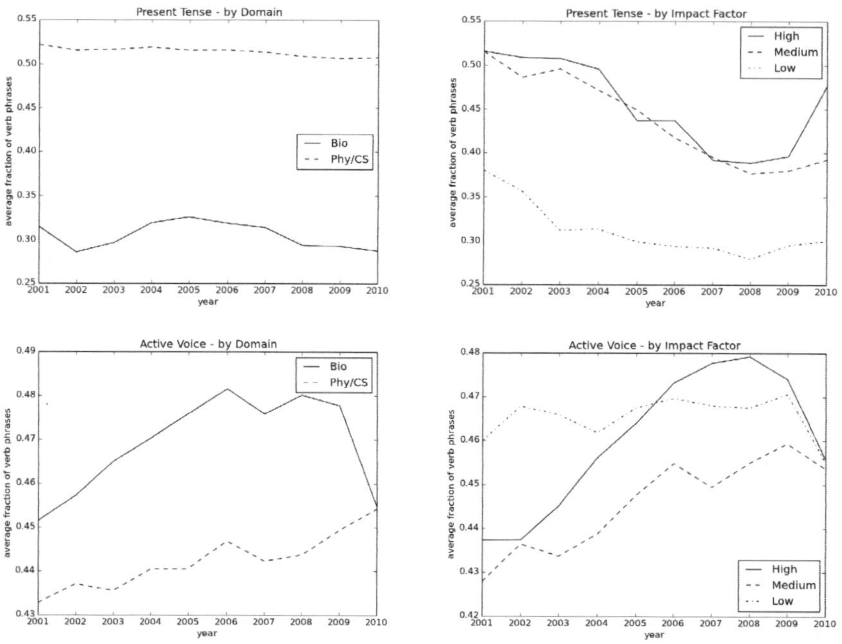


Figure 3: Illustration of average fractions of verb phrases with respect to present tense (upper figures) and active voice (lower figures) over a ten-year period. The left figures correspond to analyses with respect to domain and the right ones to analyses with respect to impact factor.

The observed high percentage of present tense and active voice verb phrases adheres to the textbook principle of lively stating one's own work. Yet, in this analysis we took into account the tense and the voice for the entire article content. To address this issue in greater depth, we intend to solely analyze abstract, introduction and conclusion in the near future.

### 3.2 Imprecision

In this section we examine indicators of scientific imprecision according to textbook literature including (i) number of citation bunches and (ii) number of relativating words.

#### 3.2.1 Citation Bunches

Statements such as "many people have been working in this research area" + a sequence of citations indicate lack of precision or insufficient dealing with the subject matter. We define a collection containing more than 3 citations as *citation bunch*. Figure 4 contains average numbers of citation bunches per article.

The left figure in Figure 4 indicates that citation bunches occur more often in the biomedical domain than in the physics/computer science domain. The right figure shows that citation bunches occur far more often in journals with a low impact factor than in those with a middle or high one.

The findings indicate that journals with a higher impact factor contain fewer citation bunches - one indicator of lack of precision. Concerning the higher numbers in the biomedical domain we intend to examine the type of scientific articles in the future; for instance, we assume that survey articles contain more citation bunches than others.

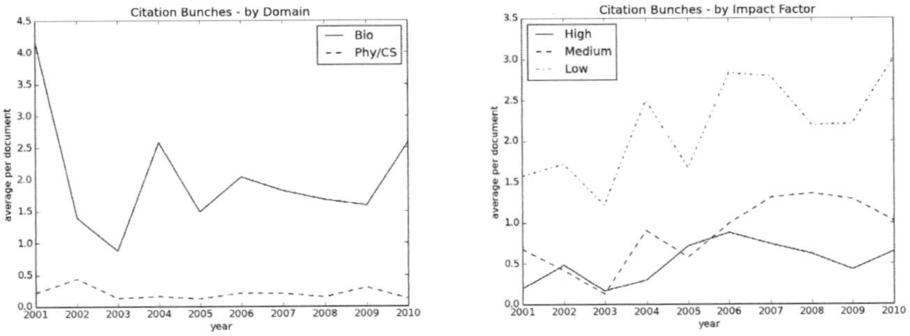


Figure 4: Illustration of averaged citation bunch counts according to domain (left) and impact factor (right)) over a ten-year period. The y-axis corresponds to the average number of citation bunches (>3 citations) per scientific article.

### 3.2.2 Usage of Relativating Words

Overusage of relativating words[10] indicates lack of precision. Reviewers may doubt an author's expertise and assurance of results if relativating words occur too frequently. Figure 5 contains average numbers of relativating words per article sentence.

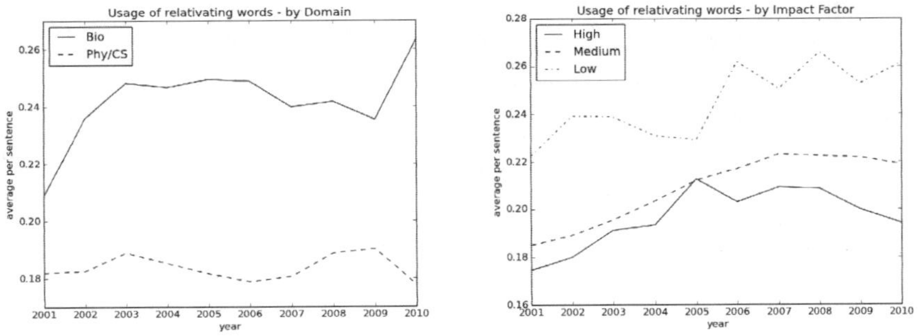


Figure 5: Illustration of relativating words usage by domain (left) and by impact factor (right). The y-axis represents the average number of relativating words per article sentence.

The left figure in Figure 5 shows that more relativating words are used in the biomedical domain than in the physics/computer science domain. In the right figure journals with a high and a middle-ranged impact factor exhibit fewer relativating words than journals with a low impact factor.

The higher usage of relativating words in the biomedical domain remains unclear and might be due to domain characteristics. Regarding the journal quality a similar behavior as in Section 3.2.1 can be observed: higher quality journals contain fewer relativating words - an indication for a higher scientific preciseness and quality.

## 4 Related Work

The analysis of academic writing originates from research areas such as linguistics and pragmatics. These areas are rather interested in studying *how* scientific articles are written instead of *what* kind of knowledge they contain.

Discourse Analysis is a modern discipline that studies amongst other things language beyond the level of a sentence taking into account the surrounding contexts as well. The detection of discourse structure in scientific documents is important for a number of tasks such as information extraction or text

[10]According to (Lebrun, 2007) relativating words include significantly, typically, generally, commonly, may/can, a number of, the majority of, substantial, probably, several, less, various, frequent, many, others, more, often, most, a few, the main.

summarization. Elements of discourse include the statement of facts, claims and hypotheses as well as the identification of methods and protocols. In this context (Liakata et al., 2012) automate the recognition of 11 categories including Hypothesis, Motivation and Result to access the scientific discourse of scientific articles. In the Partridge system, (Ravenscroft et al., 2013) build upon the automated recognition to automatically categorize articles according to their types such as Review or Case Study. (Teufel et al., 2002) used discourse analysis to summarize scientific papers. She restored the discourse context by adding the rhetorical status, for example, the scientific goal or criticism, to each sentence in an article. In a similar way, (Liakata et al., 2013) take scientific discourse into account to generate a content model for summarization purposes.

Besides analyzing the structure and organisation of entire publications (cf. (Paltridge, 2002)), there is related literature dedicated to the analysis of single (structural) elements including (i) the title or (ii) citations. The title is of particular importance often representing the first point of contact with the reader. (Haggan, 2003) investigated whether titles of scientific articles could be regarded as headlines with a clear role of informing and engaging the reader. In her work she pointed out the relation between title formulation and information advertisement. (Soler, 2007) conducted title studies in two genres (review and research papers) and in two fields (biological and social sciences). She statistically analyzed titles with respect to word count, word frequency and title construction.

Citation analysis represents one of the most widely used methods of bibliometrics which aims to quantitatively analyze academic literature. Citation analysis (cf. (Garfield, 1979)) is an expression for simply counting a scientific article's citations which can be regarded as indicator for an article's scientific impact; the more often the article is cited, the higher its academic value (cf. (Garfield, 1972)). An important part of citation analysis represents hedge detection (cf. (Lakoff, 1972)). Hedges are linguistic devices which indicate that authors do not or cannot back up their statements with facts. Hedge detection, thus, supports the distinction between facts and unreliable or uncertain information (cf. (Crompton, 1997)). Facing the continuously growing amounts of scientific articles there has been an increased interest in automating the process (cf. (Di Marco, 2006), (Farkas et al., 2007)).

## 5 Conclusion

Our paper's contribution encompasses a comparison of theoretical guidelines, i.e. "What the literature recommends?" with their practical implementations, i.e. "How authors actually write scientific articles?". We designed a framework to automatically analyze $\sim$14.000 scientific articles with respect to a selected set of writing principles.

To summarize the results: Section 3.2 shows a clear relation between journal quality and imprecision, i.e. journals with low impact factors exhibit higher numbers of imprecision indicators such as number of citation bunches and number of relativating words. In addition, the number of figures and the percentage of verb phrases in present tense tend to be higher with higher quality journals (see Section 3.1).

In respect to the domain, the results indicate writing style preferences probably due to domain characteristics, for instance, usage of more figures (see Section 3.1.2) and domain preferences, for instance, lesser usage of present tense (see Section 3.1.3).

Other interesting observations include (i) that adhering to writing principles appears to be gender independent and (ii) that using acronyms in titles is far more popular than using questions in the title (see Section 3.1.1) independent of domain and impact factor.

Our findings show that theoretical guidelines partly concur with practical implementations and thus contribute to better understand the extent to which theory guides praxis. A better understanding will contribute (i) to confirm textbook principles and (ii) to update writing principles due to good practice. In a next step we plan to extend the scale of our analyses to include several hundred thousand scientific articles as well as the complexity of our analyses to investigate issues including (i) paper skeleton, for instance, "Is there a prefered heading structure?" and (ii) usage of synonyms which hampers clarity.

## Acknowledgements

We thank Mendeley for providing the data set as well as Werner Klieber for crawling the PubMed data set. The presented work was developed within the CODE project funded by the EU FP7 (grant no. 296150). The Know-Center is funded within the Austrian COMET Program - Competence Centers for Excellent Technologies - under the auspices of the Austrian Federal Ministry of Transport, Innovation and Technology, the Austrian Federal Ministry of Economy, Family and Youth and by the State of Styria. COMET is managed by the Austrian Research Promotion Agency FFG.


## References


[Alley1996] Alley, M. 1996. *The Craft of Scientific Writing*. Springer.

[Crompton1997] Crompton, P. 1997. *Hedging in academic writing: Some theoretical problems.* English for Specific Purposes 16 (4).

[Di Marco2006] Di Marco, C., Kroon, F. and Mercer R. 2006. *Using Hedges to Classify Citations in Scientific Articles.* Computing Attitude and Affect in Text: Theory and Applications. Springer Netherlands.

[Farkas et al.2007] Farkas, R., Vincze, V., Mora, G., Csirik, J. and Szarvas, G. 2010. *The CoNLL-2010 shared task: learning to detect hedges and their scope in natural language text.* Proceedings of the Fourteenth Conference on Computational Natural Language Learning.

[Garfield1972] Garfield, E. 1972. *Citation analysis as a tool in journal evaluation.* Science (178).

[Garfield1979] Garfield, E. 1979. *Citation Indexing: Its Theory and Applications in Science, Technology, and Humanities.* John Wiley, New York, NY.

[Haggan2003] Haggan, M. 2003. *Research paper titles in literature, linguistics and science: dimensions of attraction.* Pragmatics 36 (2).

[Lakoff1972] Lakoff, G. 1972. *Hedges: A study of meaning criteria and the logic of fuzzy concepts.* Papers from the Eighth Regional Meeting, Chicago Linguistics Society Papers.

[Lebrun2007] Lebrun, J. 2007. *Scientific Writing.* World Scientific Publishing Co Pte Ltd.

[Liakata et al.2012] Liakata, M., Saha, S., Dobnik, S., Batchelor, C. and Rebholz-Schuhmann, D. 2012. *Automatic recognition of conceptualization zones in scientific articles and two life science applications.* Bioinformatics 28 (7).

[Liakata et al.2013] Liakata, M., Dobnik, S., Saha, S., Batchelor, C. and Rebholz-Schuhmann, D. 2013. *A discourse-driven content model for summarising scientific articles evaluated in a complex question answering task.* Proceedings of the Conference on Empirical Methods in Natural Language Processing.

[Klampfl et al.2013] Klampfl, S. and Kern, R. 2013. *An Unsupervised Machine Learning Approach to Body Text and Table of Contents Extraction from Digital Scientific Articles.* Research and Advanced Technology for Digital Libraries.

[Paltridge2002] Paltridge, B. 2002. *Thesis and dissertation writing: an examination of published advice and actual practice.* English for Specific Purposes 21 (2).

[Pettigrew et al.2001] Pettigrew, K. and McKechnie, L. 2001. *The use of theory in information science research.* American Society for Information Science and Technology, 52.

[Ravenscroft et al.2013] Ravenscroft, J., Liakata, M. and Clare, A. 2013. *Partridge: An Effective System for the Automatic Classification of the Types of Academic Papers.* AI-2013: The Thirty-third SGAI International Conference.

[Rubin2004] Rubin, R. 2004. *Foundations of Library and Information Science.* 2nd ed. New York: Neal-Schuman.

[Soler2007] Soler, V. 2007. *Writing titles in science: An exploratory study.* English for Specific Purposes 26 (1).

[Tas2010] Tas, E. 2010. *"In this paper I will discuss": Current trends in academic writing.* Procedia - Social and Behavioral Sciences.

[Teufel et al.2002] Teufel, S. and Marc Moens, M. 2002. *Summarizing scientific articles: experiments with relevance and rhetorical status.* Computational Linguistics 28 (4).

# Author Index

Anick, Peter, 31

Glass, Zachary, 11
Grieve-Smith, Angus, 11
Grishman, Ralph, 11

Handschuh, Siegfried, 1
He, Yifan, 11
Hu, Renfen, 40

Jin, Yaohong, 40

Kern, Roman, 48
Kröll, Mark, 48

Lévy, François, 21
Liao, Shasha, 11
Liu, Zhiying, 40

Ma, Yue, 21
Meyers, Adam, 11

Pustejovsky, James, 31

Schulze, Gunnar, 48

Tomeh, Nadi, 21

Verhagen, Marc, 31

Yang, Lijiao, 40

Zadeh, Behrang Q., 1